# DISCOVERING YOUR NATURAL TALENTS

## JOHN BRADLEY
## JAY CARTY

D0062862

**NAVPRESS** ◢

BRINGING TRUTH TO LIFE

NavPress Publishing Group

P.O. Box 35001, Colorado Springs, Colorado 80935

The Navigators is an international Christian organization. Jesus Christ gave His followers the Great
Commission to go and make disciples (Matthew
28:19). The aim of The Navigators is to help fulfill
that commission by multiplying laborers for Christ in
every nation.

NavPress is the publishing ministry of The Navigators. NavPress publications are tools to help
Christians grow. Although publications alone cannot make disciples or change lives, they can help
believers learn biblical discipleship, and apply what
they learn to their lives and ministries.

(Originally published as *Unlocking Your Sixth
Suitcase*.)

Unless otherwise identified, all Scripture in this
publication is from the *Holy Bible: New International
Version* (NIV). Copyright © 1973, 1978, 1984,
International Bible Society. Used by permission of
Zondervan Bible Publishers. Other versions used
include: the *Good News Bible: Today's English Version* (TEV), copyright © American Bible Society 1966,
1971, 1976; the *New American Standard Bible*
(NASB), © The Lockman Foundation 1960, 1962,
1963, 1968, 1971, 1972, 1973, 1975, 1977; and the
*King James Version* (KJV).

Printed in the United States of America

5 6 7 8 9 10 11 12 13 14 15 16 17 18 19 20/ 99 98 97 96 95

Since 1978, John Bradley and his career management firm, the IDAK Group, Inc., have trained and assisted hundreds of counselors, psychologists, ministry leaders, denomination executives, and college and seminary professors through the IDAK assessment process. In turn, these professionals have reached out to thousands of individuals through seminars, counseling assessment sessions, and employee training workshops.

Through the unique contribution of author and speaker Jay Carty and editor Russ Korth, John Bradley's and IDAK's assessment materials have been adapted for personal and group study.

Following are testimonials from ministry leaders, counselors, and educators who, over the years, have been uniquely helped by IDAK's principles, which are now contained in *Discovering Your Natural Talents*.

*"Our church extension department requires that all church planters complete the IDAK assessment program prior to appointment. The committee believes that the identity of the relational skills are most important for church planters. . . . The IDAK Career Match is a very valuable tool in assisting pastoral candidates to discover their strengths for ministry."*

Elvin Fast
Assistant to the Director
Northwest Conservative Baptist Association
Portland, Oregon

*"I highly recommend IDAK Career Match and the IDAK Group, Inc. I have been using their materials now for nine years and I have found them to be extremely helpful in the process of people finding their God-given capacities for excellence and how to employ them in their service for the Lord."*

Tom Lyman
Career and Organizational Consultant
Wycliff Bible Translators
Huntington Beach, California

*"I enthusiastically recommend IDAK, Inc. As compared to other systems IDAK has the ability to test for aptitudes apart from experience, which will be most useful with individuals who, simply due to their age, may have limited experience. This allows individuals to uncover latent abilities that for various reasons have never been encouraged."*

Dennis N. Baker
General Director
Conservative Baptist Association of Southern California
Los Angeles, California

*"We are so thankful to finally find the tool that we can offer to professional athletes to help them make mid-career transitions."*

Norm and Bobbe Evans
Directors
Professional Athletes Outreach
Seattle, Washington

# CONTENTS

*This book is affectionately dedicated to Dr. Grant Howard—professor, friend, and partner. Grant risked his reputation to encourage, endorse, and even sponsor the early seminar version of this manuscript in the late seventies, when much of the book's content was controversial. Grant, a deep and sincere thanks. May your tree continue to yield fruit in your season.*

# AUTHORS

*John Bradley* has specialized in mid-career-transition counseling since 1969. As president of the IDAK Group in Portland, Oregon, he has pioneered the identification and assessment of natural talents. John has trained hundreds of counselors, consultants, and psychologists in the IDAK assessment process as well as developed assessment programs for denominations, parachurch organizations, colleges, and seminaries. John earned his M.Div. at Western Seminary in Portland. His previous publications are *Christian Career Planning and IDAK Career Match*. John and the IDAK Group have developed a recognized reputation for helping individuals find their unique, God-given identity and translate that into a full-time career.

*Jay Carty,* a former NBA player for the Los Angeles Lakers, is founder and director of YES! Ministries in Corvallis,

Oregon. His ministry focuses on helping people say yes to God.

Jay speaks in churches, colleges, schools, and retreat centers across the United States and abroad, and he has appeared on numerous national radio and television programs. He has authored *Only Tens Go to Heaven, Counterattack,* and *Something's Fishy.*

# PREFACE

Our involvement with each other goes back to 1981. Jay's wife, Mary, attended one of John's "Talent Discovery" seminars. Mary, planner that she is, was beginning to prepare for an empty nest. She went home excited to tell Jay all about what she had learned. But Jay wasn't all that interested. Mary persisted anyway in trying to get Jay to go too.

At that time, Jay's career had comprised a variety of short-term positions—the longest had lasted four and a half years; the rest were less than two years each. When Mary bubbled home from John's seminar, Jay was in the midst of discovering that his current post in professional ministry was not scratching even his two-year itch.

When you are not doing what God has designed you to do, even "ministry" isn't fulfilling.

Mary finally got Jay to a seminar. He caught the concepts and went a step further, pursuing a career aptitude assessment from John at John's IDAK Group office. (The meaning of IDAK is "unique identity." ID comes from the word *identity*; AK is from an ancient Hebrew derivative, which translates as "unique" or "uniqueness.") They became friends through the process, and then added professional teamwork to friendship. Their work together began to blossom.

Jay's experience of discovery led him to start a new outreach, YES! Ministries, structured around his natural talents and a better understanding of how he is gifted by God. You might say he found his niche. And in the process, his relationship to Mary was enriched and his hobbies were enhanced.

This positive ripple effect is a common result of discovering God-given talents. John's and Jay's experience in counseling and speaking has put them in touch with hundreds of individuals seeking a better understanding of their God-given strengths. It's amazing how many people are struggling in this area. When they receive help in discovering their natural God-given strengths, they tend to blossom spiritually, professionally, and personally.

The concepts in this book have worked for them, their families, and the thousands of people who have gone through this material. That's why they got together to write this book. The author's and publisher's prayer is that this approach will equip you for a more rewarding purpose in your life journey.

# INTRODUCTION:
# WHO SAID I WAS GOING
# ON A TRIP?

Like it or not, your life is moving in some direction. Whether you are a weary traveler or an airplane pilot, eventually you will end up somewhere. But, you say, "Stop, I want to get off." . . . Maybe just for a moment. Okay, let's stop and think for a moment. While you're resting, think of three well-known people you admire.

Don't get back on your tiresome journey again—stop and think of three people. If you follow politics, perhaps one of the people you admire is a political leader. Or you may think of an author, or a theologian, or a musician, or an artist, or a sports figure. You may admire one of the Nobel Peace Prize winners or a popular Christian leader.

Now consider the life journey these three people have taken. Consider the level of excellence they have demonstrated. Compare it to the level of excellence you have achieved up to this point in your life journey.

Have these individuals achieved a greater level of excellence than you have?

Do you expect that someday your level of excellence in your field will be as great as theirs in their fields?

People often laugh when they are asked these questions. They think it's obvious that they'll never achieve that level of excellence, so the question is humorous. Yes, and sadly, they get right back on their wearisome journey.

But we're not joking. We believe that you can achieve a level of excellence in your life journey as great as that of anyone else, famous or not. Remember:

*Achieving the same level of excellence does not mean you will necessarily gain the same level of accomplishment.*

Nobel Peace Prize winners are few. And most of us will never have our picture on a magazine cover.

But realizing excellence in your life journey will mean reaching a level of mastery with the aptitudes God has given you. This is not only a possibility, it is an expectation.

## EXPECTING THE EXCELLENCE
## YOU WERE BORN TO ACHIEVE

Scripture sets out this expectation of excellence in our life journey through several passages. The writer to the Hebrews, for example, encourages us to follow the example of heroes in the faith and "run with endurance the race [journey] that is set before us" (12:1). Each of those heroes had his or her individual race—and you have yours. No matter what your particular journey is, you can race through it to excellence, because you're not in competition with others—only with yourself.

Paul also uses the image of running a race to encourage us to excellence. He told the Corinthians, "Do you remember how, on a race track, every competitor runs, but only one wins the prize? Well, you ought to run with your minds fixed on winning the prize." (See 1 Corinthians 9:24.) Paul's teaching indicates that *each* of us should expect excellence as our life journey goal.

Certainly Paul's own life illustrated this personal striving. He was not boasting when he said shortly before he died, "As for me, I feel that the last drops of my life are being poured out for God. The glorious fight that God gave me I have fought, the course that I was set, I have finished, and I have kept the faith" (2 Timothy 4:7). Paul's life journey counted for something worthwhile.

Perhaps it might help you to think of excellence as *maximizing God's endowment in you.* This understanding brings it down to earth; excellence is no longer the rare accomplishment of an ambitious few. The way we achieve excellence varies as widely as the abilities God has given each of us.

We have a clear picture of this individualized achievement in Jesus' parable of the nobleman who distributed his wealth among three servants before taking an extended trip (Matthew 25:14-30). Each servant was entrusted with an amount of money in proportion to his ability to manage it. When the master returned, he didn't rub his hands together and exclaim, "Well, boys, whichever one of you made me the most money will now get the prize." Instead, he rewarded his servants according to how well they had carried out his orders to invest their sum. Two of the servants doubled their original amount and were praised; the third had zero return and was punished.

The one who turned five talents into ten could be compared to those famous achievers you admire. The one who turned two talents into four is probably more like the rest of us. But notice that both of them received exactly the same honor from their master. Condemnation was reserved for the lone servant who played it safe and buried his one talent in the ground rather than risk losing it. This parable shows us that excellence means *doing your best with what you've been given*—not living up to some arbitrary, across-the-board standard of achievement.

## FINDING YOUR OWN PATH

Are you questioning how realistic it is to expect excellence in your life journey? Perhaps you're trying to walk down someone else's path. If so, you'll probably find it rough going.

When you concentrate on the talents God has put within you, you'll start charting your personal path to excellence. Identifying these talents and learning how to make the best use of them for the short *and* long haul is what this book is all about.

We'll be leading you through a process that will help you realize you have the ability to achieve excellence, to make a difference with your life, to accomplish something noteworthy. We're not trying to motivate you to "think big," or to pump you with enthusiasm. *The attributes that will lead you to excellence are in you right now.* All you have to do is discover them and commit yourself to developing them. This is what we will help you to do in the course of this book.

As you go through this discovery process, you'll probably start clearing away the fog of confusion that blinds so many of us to the path. Think of what happens in churches when people don't know how to say no to jobs that aren't right for them. Someone lacking in supervisory talents becomes the Sunday school superintendent, and we wonder why the program is slipping. The mistake here is squeezing people into existing slots rather than adapting positions to suit the talents of individuals who are then free to achieve excellence.

The same thing can happen in marriage relationships, friendships, employment positions, even recreational activities. We can create stereotypes for ourselves and for others that are contrary to how God has gifted us.

A wife's work can be reduced to a maintenance role—

someone who washes, cooks, drives, cleans, and is always on call—in ignorance of her need to grow in the areas where she's gifted. A husband must come equipped to be a mechanic, builder, explorer, trainer, entrepreneur—when instead he's a musician, an artist, a poet. How ironic that many of us don't know our own road to excellence, but we try to manipulate others onto paths we've marked out for them.

This conflict occurs just as easily at work. An energetic, athletic person is assigned to a project requiring highly detailed bookkeeping procedures. A creative individual is restricted by a long list of rules, and her response appears to be open rebellion. The top faculty professor becomes the college president and burns out with the management responsibilities, not realizing that some promotions lead to an early "mid-life crisis."

Think of how most of us spend our leisure time. Yielding to pressures from business, family, or tradition, we pursue recreational activities that may be contrary to our natural talents. We get so used to golfing, water skiing, camping, or playing bridge that we don't realize we've stopped growing and that possibly these activities are a source of subliminal stress.

Much of this confusion can be traced to this commonly believed half-truth: "You can succeed at anything you set your mind to do." This thinking can work for some; but for most, it creates a lot of blisters, headaches, and ulcers along life's journey.

## SOMEONE ELSE'S PATH
## CAN LEAD TO YOUR DEAD END

Maybe you can succeed at anything and maybe you can't. It depends upon what you're shooting for and how you define success. The problem with asserting that you can succeed at whatever you put your mind to lies in the suggestion that you *ought* to attempt success in whatever goal you establish.

That belief can lead to unnecessary burnout.

George is a classic case of following someone else's path into his dead end. He was a top salesperson in a medical equipment firm. His employer contacted John's office for help when George's sales performance suddenly dropped dramatically. George's boss, who had been planning to promote George to a higher level of sales management, was shocked. There had been no change in the economy, no new developments in the industry—no external reasons that could explain such a drastic change.

As John began to explore George's background to assess his aptitudes, he found some of George's favorite activities were data processing, reading, writing, and research. Parties were one of his least favorite activities. These and other clues indicated that George's natural inclination was to work alone for long periods of time in project research or independent study.

George also sought opportunities to comfort and encourage others, and he delighted in waiting on them. When George was being himself and doing his favorite activities, there appeared to be no consistent pattern indicating salesmanship as an area of strength.

You may be wondering how George ever became the top salesperson in his company. He did it by pursuing diligently his primary goal of attaining a high income. He regularly devoted sixty to eighty hours per week, sometimes more, to his job. His family life revolved around his work even to the point of deciding not to have children. George's single-minded determination and zeal enabled him to achieve an award-winning sales record during his earlier years.

George had no idea of the price tag to this appearance of success. In his five years with the medical equipment firm, he had reached the pinnacle of his field. But he had spent all his energy doing it, and he found that he could no longer put up the front. The outgoing sales facade was not him. He burned out.

Now George was in jeopardy of losing not only his prize

of high financial reward, but perhaps even his employment. The threat of demotion compelled him to question his identity, purpose, and future.

## DEFINING SUCCESS

By some definitions, George was achieving excellence when he was the top salesperson. But according to our definition, he wasn't. He was going against his God-given aptitudes in pursuit of a misguided ambition.

It would be easy to find fault with George's materialistic goal. Certainly his objectives did need to change. But before we point to that as the source of George's problem, let's remember that this same scenario occurs in many other contexts. For example, well-intentioned individuals enter the pastorate because their primary goal is to minister to people, but they don't have the natural talents required for the position of pastor. A commendable goal that is out of harmony with natural talents can result in the same kind of burnout that George experienced.

In fact, turning away from a commitment to a commendable goal can be especially difficult. Many assume that wholehearted effort will produce success. They consider it godly to pursue such a goal with complete abandon. "Look at the dedication, the sacrifices, the intensity," they will say. But we would like to suggest that *many times this high degree of energy is required not because the task is so hard but because the person is not suited to the task.*

Failing to attain a lofty goal can be a worse setback than simply changing course. Many people assume that the reason for such failure is a lack of commitment or dedication to God. This can produce a false sense of guilt.

You are truly successful when your efforts are in harmony with the natural talents God has given you. When you strive for excellence according to this definition of success, you'll discover that your hard work, determination, and sacrifices will bear fruit. Instead of expending excessive amounts of energy trying to live up to your responsibilities, you'll find that your hard work isn't really all that difficult. You'll start achieving that level of excellence you've seen in others.

## HOW TO LOVE WHAT YOU DO AND DO WHAT YOU LOVE

The following chapters will help you use the resources packed in one of your suitcases for your life journey ahead. We'll help you unlock your "sixth suitcase"—the key to understanding how God has gifted you— and learn how to use its contents to put you on your own path to personal excellence.

You'll be asked to respond to a variety of questions. Relax—this is not a test. Enjoy using these questions as prompters to open up certain aspects of yourself you might otherwise overlook. Feel free to change your responses at any time.

Remember that this book is an important step toward knowing what you're best suited to do and being motivated to go after it. It is not a guaranteed tool kit or survival bag that will detail exactly what you should do in every area of life. This is a discovery process, not an exact science. But we have built in personal validation exercises to help you confirm your conclusions. So be reasonable in your expectations, and then look forward to what you'll discover about yourself.

We highly recommend using this book in the context of a small group. (See the study guide sections at the end of each chapter, "Reflections for Your Journey.") A group can help you clarify thoughts and ideas you may be overlooking or subconsciously avoiding. If possible, find a group of five or six others and go through the process together. If you can't, press ahead on your own, perhaps bouncing your ideas off a trusted friend from time to time.

You are about to find out how to use your God-given talents to achieve a standard of excellence in your life journey. May this discovery lead you to a path where you can honor God with the strengths He has given you.

# PART ONE

# EXPLORING YOUR SIXTH SUITCASE

# ONE

# DISCOVERING YOUR NATURAL TALENTS

wo of life's most important journey questions are, "Who am I?" and "What am I trying to accomplish with my life?"

These issues, self concept and life goals, are intricately connected. In order to form a healthy response to these questions, we need to understand these issues in harmony with each other and with reality.

How do we harmonize self-concept with life goals? Let's start by looking at the first question, "Who am I?"

Over the years we've listened to people describe their attributes—"I'm the kind of person who . . . ." We've heard a colorful variety of terms for strengths and capabilities. Many people repeat the expressions their parents told them, or a recent job performance rating, or the results of a psychological test. Others rehearse their achievements in school, in sports, at church or in the community. Others depict themselves by their job title, "manager," or their profession, "lawyer."

These varied responses consistently fall into about five general categories that most people use to describe their strengths. We call them "suitcases": Each one carries important necessities for your life journey—achievements, skills, status, personality, and everything else that makes you the unique individual you are.

## #1—THE WORK CASE

This suitcase contains your life journey achievements earned "on the job." It includes all the hands-on-related tasks you have carried out, from the first lawn mowing or baby-sitting job all the way up to your present position.

Some of these jobs are not salaried positions, such as home responsibilities, church work, or community service. Some are routine jobs (e.g., household chores); others may occur only once in your life (e.g., lead role in a dramatic presentation).

This suitcase contains the "I have done . . ." statements.

## #2—THE SCHOOL CASE

The second suitcase holds your life journey education and training achievements. It's filled with your knowledge skills. You may have acquired these through formal education, informal reading on your own, attending lectures or conferences, or conducting your own research.

This suitcase contains the "I have a degree in . . ." and "I know about . . ." statements.

## #3—THE PERSONALITY CASE

The third suitcase is filled with the inner qualities of your life—temperament, character, disposition, and personality characteristics. These contents combine the raw material that God put in you with your conditioning in family, school, church environment, network of friends, and your own self-discipline.

Notice that you have less immediate selection and control of the contents of this case compared to the first two suitcases. When people describe themselves according to these qualities, they tend to assume certain lifelong patterns in their personal makeup. Over the last twenty years several tests (such as the TJTA, MMPI, or Myers-Briggs) have become popular that identify and give names to these patterns. Many people now characterize themselves in such terms as a "type A personality," "choleric," "direct-expressive," or "an ENTJ." They simply categorize descriptions of an individual's personal tendencies.

This suitcase contains many (but certainly not all) of your "I am the type of person who . . ." statements.

## #4—THE INTERESTS CASE

The fourth suitcase contains interests, concerns, attractions, and fascinations that you have collected in your life journey. Some of these are still with you and others have passed.

Here we're examining your taste in food and music, your recreation and hobbies, your entertainment, your attraction to certain colors, and anything else that delights you. You might talk of the thrill of riding roller coasters, the challenge of flying an airplane, or your love of travel.

This suitcase is a rather large one. It is continually expanding with new things as you're exposed to them. It contains the "I like . . ." statements.

## #5—THE VALUES CASE

In the fifth suitcase you carry all that is important to you, now and in the future of your life journey. These are deep-seated convictions, motivations, and commitments. This is what you esteem, prize, and regard—the things you consider worthy, significant, or of consequence. These values guide the decisions you make and provide the reasons you make them. The basis for marriage and parenting, your Christian beliefs, the attitude you have toward the Word of God—all of these fit into the values suitcase.

This case is not as large as your interests suitcase because it does not add or lose items as quickly. Normally it is a gradual, growing process. However, when there is a major change in your life, such as death of a loved one, divorce, major illness or injury, or job loss, you may reevaluate and adjust your values more sharply.

This suitcase has your "I believe . . ." statements.

## SUITCASE SUMMARY

| NAME | CONTENTS | COMMON EXPRESSION |
| --- | --- | --- |
| Work Case | Achievements earned from work, activities, duties, services | "I can do . . ." "I have done . . ." |
| School Case | Degrees, certificates, information, formulas | "I know about . . ." |
| Personality Case | The inner you, temperament, character | "I am the type who . . ." |
| Interests Case | Tastes, attractions, inclinations | "I like . . ." |
| Values Case | Convictions, beliefs, faith | "I believe . . ." |

To illustrate these categories of personal attributes, let's sketch them out for two individuals. Consider these profiles of Bill and Sarah Smith to help you distinguish between these five "suitcases."

*Bill's Work Case*
Since his graduation from college twelve years ago, Bill has been employed as a design engineer and project manager for a corporation that manufactures aerospace components. Last year he was the chairman of the United Way

campaign. He is also active as a trustee at his church and as a coach for Little League baseball.

*Bill's School Case*
Bill has a B.S. in electrical engineering and is completing graduate work toward an M.B.A. He has attended many work-related seminars and several church retreats and Bible conferences. He watches public television documentaries exploring foreign cultures and reads *Scientific American* magazine. Two years ago he went on a lecture tour of the Holy Land. He regularly listens to self-improvement cassettes while driving to work.

*Bill's Personality Case*
A personality survey indicates that Bill is loyal, trustworthy, stable, not impulsive, and makes decisions objectively, considering all the facts. He is quiet, and sometimes moody. He tends to become depressed when faced with disappointments.

*Bill's Interests Case*
Bill loves the outdoors, especially water sports such as water-skiing, windsurfing, and sailing. He likes baseball, roast beef, and contemporary jazz. His favorite color is blue.

*Bill's Values Case*
Bill is a deeply committed Christian. He reflects on the Bible when making decisions. He has a deep loyalty to his wife and family and a strong drive to master challenges put in front of him. He seeks leadership roles and expects his work to meet a standard of excellence.

*Sarah's Work Case*
Sarah is a floral designer and homemaker. She works half-time at a florist shop. As a homemaker, she focuses on gardening, interior design, photography, and piano playing; she also designs remodeling and landscaping projects. Sarah has taught aerobics and women's Bible study classes. She is active in the PTA and in environmental causes.

*Sarah's School Case*
Sarah has a teaching credential in elementary education with a specialty in art. She regularly reads magazines related to architectural and home design. She participates in a women's Bible study and has attended several seminars on Christian growth. Sarah has completed non-credit courses at a community college in home remodeling, furniture upholstery, family finances, and photography. She took a lecture tour of the Holy Land.

*Sarah's Personality Case*
Sarah tends to be a stable individual who is disciplined to complete tasks but also capable of spontaneity. She is tolerant of the differences in other people and sympathetic to the needs of those who are less fortunate. She tends to have some difficulty acknowledging her own inconsistencies.

*Sarah's Interests Case*
Sarah loves the theater as well as the outdoors—especially hiking, backpacking, and wilderness exploration. She enjoys doing handicraft projects to give as presents. Her favorite color is crimson red.

*Sarah's Values Case*
Sarah is deeply committed to pursuing a lifestyle that reflects the Bible's teaching. Her highest priority is her family, including home-schooling her children. She also believes in giving volunteer time to worthy community activities. She feels strongly about caring for her elderly parents and visits them regularly. She also looks after an adopted grandmother from church.

## THE SIXTH SUITCASE

You can see from the example of Bill and Sarah that these five categories do a fairly good job of covering the territory of personal attributes.

But we want to draw your attention to a sixth area that we feel is often forgotten or ignored—and so it's exactly the area that needs the most attention in answering the questions, "Who am I?" and "What am I trying to accomplish with my life?"

This neglected suitcase does not eclipse the value of the other five. They are all important. In recent years many people have been particularly helped by a greater understanding of the contents of their personality case. Their new insights have enabled them to accept themselves and others without becoming complacent. We applaud most of these helps. Our desire is to add another support through unlocking the sixth suitcase.

*The sixth suitcase contains the inherent talents God selected to be part of you when He created you.* We might say it contains the "I have a natural talent for . . ." or "I am particularly good at . . ." statements. You came into this world with this suitcase already full. You may discover more about it, but you won't be adding or losing contents. If you were adopted, came from a dysfunctional home, or are a recovering alcoholic, your natural talents are still intact the way God gave them to you at birth.

*All those attributes that are uniquely God-given, not acquired by effort, are in this sixth suitcase.* Of course in order to achieve excellence with these talents, you must develop them. But they often show up when you begin putting them to use in a particular context—triggering the comment from someone observing you, "You took to that like a duck to water!"

The duck analogy is a good one. Let's take it a little further. God created ducks to be in water. They come equipped with feathers, feet, and a preferred diet that all suggest an aquatic habitat. You also come equipped with talents that are designed best for certain applications. Your "feathers," your "feet," and your preferences are gifts God has provided for you. It's your choice whether you will do something with your talents or not.

*Recognizing the relationship between your natural talents and your life journey goals is critically important to answering the questions "Who am I?" and "What am I trying to accomplish?"*

When you don't understand what's in your sixth suitcase, you will almost certainly step into the subtle trap of establishing your ambitions based only on your first five suitcases.

This trap is so subtle that it may not be evident to you yet. Read on to see how it can snare people.

## THE MISCALCULATION TRAP

When we attempt to define our life goals, passion, or "calling," most of us build on our interests and our values. If we're interested in aviation and financial security is high on our values list, we might set our sights on becoming a commercial pilot for a major airline. Or if encouraging others' spiritual growth is high on our values list, we might decide to pursue a discipleship ministry. How we go about this ministry might depend on our interests. An interest in counseling could lead one person into a master's program; a high interest in preaching could lead another into seminary.

But values and interests are not enough to confirm the wisdom of such a decision. The potential pilot has yet to test his aptitude for flying. The would-be counselor will be successful only if she is gifted in such personal interaction. And an interest in preaching combined with a dedication to discipleship does not automatically qualify one for the myriad demands of pastoring a congregation.

The trap of miscalculating what we have to offer and where we ought to give it opens wide when we do not factor in natural abilities along with interests and values. One of John's clients, whom we'll call Richard, illustrates this fundamental miscalculation.

When he was a college sophomore, Richard decided that he wanted to become a dentist. His parents had not pushed him in this direction, but he knew they wanted him to "make something of himself"—that is, attain some professional status. They were delighted with his decision and did all they could to help him.

With his good grades, Richard had no problem getting into dental school and completed it on schedule. But after graduation Richard repeatedly failed the dental licensing exam. The reason turned out to be that he lacked the necessary hand and finger dexterity to manipulate delicate dental instruments.

But Richard refused to give up his ambition, even after he was forced to admit his lack of natural talent in this area. He finally entered the military, where he was allowed to practice dentistry.

When Richard came to IDAK for counseling, he felt that he was a failure. John's first step was to help him see the difference between being a failure and failing to become a dentist.

Some of Richard's misguided feelings were fostered by well-meaning friends who attempted to encourage him with the assurance, "You can pass the exam next time." This kind of support compounded the problem because it ignored reality. Deep down Richard knew he did not have the natural talent to use those tools. The disparity between his ambition and his natural talents had been like the San Andreas plates—it was building tension and stress toward an inevitable earthquake.

Richard finally admitted that a major motivation in his desire to become a dentist was the image of being someone important and making a lot of money. This area needed reworking.

Once Richard had realigned his motives to reflect scriptural values, he was willing to consider an alternate career. The results of John's counseling assessment indicated that he was very gifted with numerical calculation and well suited to be an insurance underwriter or research statistician.

Richard had previously rejected office administrative positions as inferior in status to a career as a dentist. But after reevaluating his motives and gaining confidence in his natural strengths, he accepted the idea of a career change and became an insurance underwriter.

Richard took to this new job like our proverbial duck. His feelings about himself changed, his stress level dropped sharply, and his income even increased.

## TELLTALE SIGNS OF A BAD MATCH

Like the instability along the San Andreas fault, the subterranean tension produced by a bad match of ambitions and natural talents shows itself in above-ground signs. Here are some of the most notable in people experiencing this kind of stress:

- They are constantly pushing to keep up.
- They are consistently tired.
- They talk of burnout.
- They are defensive about the work they do.
- They are either not willing to acknowledge, or actively critical of, the accomplishments of others.
- They are excessively competitive.
- They are constantly trying to out-maneuver others.
- They are frustrated by lack of achievement.
- They are depressed because they have tried so hard and have nothing to show for it.
- They are criticized as being a phony by those who are closest to them.
- They are rejected by their children, who see a double standard.
- They are hard to get to know.
- They are afraid others will find out who they really are.

- They look for ways to impress others with clothes, money, or association with famous people.
- They are desperate because they lack the approval of their spouse.

You will rarely find someone who evidences all or even most of these symptoms. And most of us exhibit some of them from time to time, because we all have our insecurities. But when a cluster of these conditions forms a significant pattern, it indicates a problem.

You may notice that three foundational sources of trouble underlie the items on the above list: (1) distorted self-concept; (2) excessive energy required to keep up with others; (3) fear of failure.

An inaccurate or inadequate self-concept, especially in the area of natural talents, can lead to establishing unrealistic ambitions. Then the pursuit of unrealistic goals can lead to further distortions of self-concept. So this particular source of trouble crops up at the root and in the fruit of unrealistic ambition.

The other two sources of trouble feed each other: the more energy we have to put in at something that doesn't come naturally to us anyway, the more we fear failing at it; the more we fear failure, the harder we work to stave it off.

Ducks do not work hard at learning to swim. When we're operating at a frenetic energy level just to stay afloat, we need to ask ourselves if we've made a bad match of our ambitions and our talents—we're trying to build a bridge over the Grand Canyon.

It would be a wonderful ambition to build such a bridge. Imagine the view of the canyon from the middle—incredible! The bridge would open a new world to tourists: the other rim. For instead of driving 220 miles around the canyon, you could cross it in only six miles. It would attract thousands from around the world; no doubt feasibility studies would indicate financial success. No, you can't go wrong planning a bridge to span the Grand Canyon—except for one minor detail. It is unrealistic.

Today thousands of us are building our air bridges across a personal Grand Canyon. Our unrealistic ambition, based on ignorance of our natural talents, leads us into a frenzy of high-energy activity that tries to fill our work and school cases—more experience and more education. This produces more stress than accomplishment. The more energy we invest, the more threatening the failure. All that work with so little to show for it—what will others say or think if we don't succeed? What will we think of ourselves?

## TEST YOUR STRESS LEVEL

Are you trying to stretch too far to realize your goals? Do you wonder if you're building a bridge in thin air over an uncrossable chasm?

Try the "I'm tired of . . ." exercise to test your current stress level. It's fast and simple. Get a piece of paper, something to write with, and a watch or clock. In two minutes, finish the sentence "I'm tired of . . ." with as many phrases as come to your mind. Your only restriction is that your finished sentence must be true. Stop after two minutes.

The list of statements you now have is a catalog of your frustrations. Because of the two-minute time limit, you've probably listed the ones that plague you the most.

There is no science to interpreting your list. Common sense should give you some insight into the nature of your fatigue. A statement like "I'm tired of the neighbor revving up his noisy car early in the morning" indicates your frustration is not with yourself. This statement is not a reflection of air-bridge-building fatigue.

Some statements may require further investigation before you can categorize them. For example, if you wrote "I'm tired of battling finances," it could be due to poor budgeting, a lack of biblical values regarding money, unrealistic financial expectations, or several other possibilities.

But if you wrote "I'm tired of making phone calls,"

and phoning is an integral part of your work, it's likely that you're experiencing work-related stress from excessive energy required to fulfill an unrealistic ambition—in short, from air-bridge building.

Please don't jump to the expectation that all you have to do is discover your natural talents to get rid of your frustrations. Or to eliminate all your stressful activities. After all, ducks swim easily in water, but they still have to walk on land—and they do that poorly. Such waddling is a normal and inevitable cause of frustration.

But although ducks can't eliminate land excursions, they don't make backpacking a major part of their activity. You can't eliminate your waddling, nor should you attempt to do so. Just don't make it a primary activity. We suggest the sixty-forty rule: spend at least 60 percent of your time in your areas of strength as indicated by your natural talents, and no more than 40 percent of your time in areas of non-strength.

A non-strength does not excuse you from developing a degree of competence in that area. You may not be gifted as a supervisor, but if you have children, you do need to supervise them. Learning how to oversee your children is not air-bridge building; selecting a career goal to be a department store manager is.

## WHAT KEEPS YOU FROM UNLOCKING YOUR SIXTH SUITCASE

Some of us never get around to unlocking our sixth suitcase—or if we do get that far, we stop short of internalizing the contents. What keeps us from recognizing and building on our God-given abilities?

Over the years we have stumbled into numerous obstacles from the very people we were attempting to help. As you look at the following list of hurdles to discovering and applying natural talents, consider whether they might apply to you. Sometimes the best way to get an obstacle out of your path is simply to recognize that it's there. Here is what we've discovered keeps most people from utilizing their sixth suitcase:

*Fear of Losing a Lifelong Passion*
Many of us cherish an ambition that is more than a passing fancy or a calculated decision based on weighing pros and cons. It is a lifelong passion. We can't tolerate any suggestion that our ambition is unrealistic or out of harmony with our makeup because we can't bear the thought of giving up this goal. We start denying obvious conclusions in an effort to protect our passion.

Our cherished ambitions usually reflect a combination of our interests and values. These are both important and good. But they can't take the place of talent. In most cases, learning about our natural talents will not eliminate or change our lifelong passion, but instead open the door to its fulfillment. Knowing our natural talents allows us to redirect our aims to a realistic, accomplishable goal.

For example, we have counseled clergy who had a passion for ministry but were experiencing burnout because they were attempting job duties that did not match their talents. For them, the ministry had become another exercise in building a bridge across the Grand Canyon. They had different talents than those required by their daily grind. When these pastors saw how they could use their natural talents in church ministry with adjustments to their job description, their passion was fulfilled and revived.

> No part of the process in this book will assault your passion. But it *will* assault the notion that your passion determines your giftedness.

*Failure to Recognize Strengths*
None of us likes to focus on what we *can't* do. But if we're not sure about what we *can* do, we're likely to feel very threatened by the prospect of acknowledging those areas

in which we lack strengths. When we're not sure what we're really good at, we may retreat in fear of finding out that we just don't *have* any talents.

But God has given each of us unique talent gifts. And once we grasp this truth, we'll be able to relax and examine ourselves honestly. We'll want to let go of our misconceptions and begin embracing our case of natural talents.

Our intention is to help you find your strengths, not expose your weaknesses. As you go through this book you will be discovering personal strengths in the way you communicate, the way you relate, and the way you function. You also will learn how you lead others. As you focus on these abilities, you'll build confidence and self-acceptance with them. You'll be able to acknowledge your God-given limitations, because you won't be failing to recognize your strengths.

*Acquired Prejudices*
Throughout our lives we are continually exposed to influences that shape our value system. Along the way we can acquire prejudices toward certain people or subjects without being aware that we are developing unfounded attitudes or false judgments.

Some of these prejudices, such as racial bias, are morally wrong and need to be corrected using the teaching of Scripture. Others can simply be mistaken generalizations or shallow assumptions—such as "all lawyers are crafty" or "people who drive a Mercedes are materialistic."

Unless we acknowledge and correct these prejudices, they can interfere with our self-image and life goals, steering us away from certain career fields.

Some of these prejudices take the form of false judgments we make about ourselves. The strong emphasis in school on verbal communication has conditioned many of us to believe that good communication is limited to the correct use of the spoken or written word. As we will see, there are other valid modes of communicating—art and music, for example. But acquired prejudices can make those who excel in other forms of communication feel inferior to those with strong verbal skills.

*Testiphobia*
We coined the word *testiphobia* to describe the fear of taking a test. People who have this fear are often reluctant to engage in self-evaluation exercises because they feel too much like a test. And a test, in their frame of reference, is a threat.

Testiphobiacs can take many forms. Some are afraid of not "getting the right answer," and can spend a long time trying to second-guess what is expected of them. Others value accuracy and detail so much they're never finished with their responses.

## DISCOVERING YOUR TALENTS

Now that you are aware of potential obstacles, you are ready to begin your steps to discovery. You are moving closer to unlocking your sixth suitcase.

In the following section we'll be introducing you to our time-tested "Talent Discovery Guide." This is a specially adapted version of IDAK's talent assessment process, which has helped thousands of people. It's not a test, but it does have blanks to fill in—and that's close enough to trigger testiphobia in some people. If you fall into this category, please read on. The purpose of this exercise is to help *you* learn about you.

We use the "Talent Discovery Guide" to help people recall the kinds of activities they've engaged in from their teen years on. It's easy to forget what you did years earlier unless someone jogs your memory.

Approach this guide in a relaxed manner. A few discrepancies between memory and reality will not negate its overall value. Don't be overwhelmed by it. Use it and have fun with it.  .

## THE TALENT DISCOVERY GUIDE

**A.** The following list is designed to help you recall past experiences and activities from your freshman year of high school to the present. Review this list and place a check by each activity you have enjoyed as a past experience.

---

HOBBIES/ACTIVITIES
- ❏ Photography
- ❏ Building Models
- ❏ Designing Clothing
- ❏ Sewing
- ❏ Needlework
- ❏ Interior Decorating
- ❏ Gardening, Lawn Care
- ❏ Flower Arranging
- ❏ Fine Arts, Painting
- ❏ Sculpting
- ❏ Cooking
- ❏ Reading
- ❏ Creative Writing
- ❏ Speaking to Groups
- ❏ Short Wave Radio/C.B.
- ❏ Electronics
- ❏ Metalworking, Jewelry
- ❏ Home Remodeling
- ❏ Construction
- ❏ Car Repair
- ❏ Arts and Crafts
- ❏ Games: Chess, Bridge, Monopoly, etc.
- ❏ Sports
- ❏ Collecting Things
- ❏ Traveling
- ❏ Antiques
- ❏ Woodworking
- ❏ Crossword Puzzles
- ❏ Word Games
- ❏ Camping/Hiking/Backpacking
- ❏ Hunting, Fishing, Trapping
- ❏ Discussion Groups
- ❏ Concerts: Symphony/Jazz/ Rock
- ❏ Volunteer Teaching
- ❏ Driving/Operating Vehicles: Auto/ Motorcycle, etc.
- ❏ Pets: Fish, Cat, Dog
- ❏ Ceramics, Leathertooling
- ❏ Read Business Magazines
- ❏ Political Campaigns
- ❏ Attend Auctions, Sales
- ❏ Teacher's Aide/Tutor
- ❏ Write Letters to Publications
- ❏ Art Galleries/Exhibits
- ❏ Play on Team/Athletic Activities
- ❏ Cut Friends' Hair/Apply Makeup
- ❏ Serve Food at Receptions
- ❏ Member of Music Group (Folk, Country, etc.)
- ❏ Boating
- ❏ Flying
- ❏ Horseback Riding
- ❏ Upholstering
- ❏ Make Posters for Activity
- ❏ Dramatic Performance
- ❏ Member of a Study Group
- ❏ Individual Study/Research of a Topic
- ❏ Movies/Films
- ❏ Writing Literary Material
- ❏ Singing as Performer
- ❏ Playing Musical Instrument
- ❏ Conducting Music
- ❏ Writing Music
- ❏ Chemistry Experiments
- ❏ Time with Family and/or Friends
- ❏ Appliance Repair
- ❏ Listening to Friends (Counseling)
- ❏ Rearranging Home/Furniture
- ❏ Budgeting Finances/Checkbook
- ❏ Researching a Subject
- ❏ Coaching a Team
- ❏ Arranging Social Gathering
- ❏ Computer Work
- ❏ Attending Plays/Drama

❑ Acting in Dramatic Group
❑ Dancing: Social, Ballet, Jazz, etc.
❑ Promoting Group Activities
❑ Graphic Design, Cartoons, Signs
❑ Watching TV
❑ Entertaining Guests
❑ Dabbling in Stocks, Investments, Real Estate
❑ Bargaining ("Swapping")
❑ Exercising
❑ Computer Games, Video Games
❑ Other _____

COMMUNITY ACTIVITIES
❑ Service Clubs, etc.
❑ Junior Chamber of Commerce
❑ Civic Volunteer
❑ Head Start, etc.
❑ United Way, March of Dimes
❑ Neighborhood Groups
❑ Political Campaigns
❑ Parent/Teachers Association
❑ Christian Business Clubs
❑ Civil Air Patrol
❑ Environmental Group
❑ Consumer Group
❑ Hospital Volunteer
❑ Museum/Historical Society
❑ Scouting Troop
❑ Rescue Squad/Volunteer Fire Dept.
❑ Fund-Raising Activities
❑ Care for Shut-ins
❑ Other _____

SCHOOL ACTIVITIES/SUBJECTS
❑ Future Farmers of America/4-H
❑ Foreign Exchange Student
❑ Student Government
❑ Athletics: Individual, Team
❑ Cheerleader/Pep Squad
❑ Drama, Theatre
❑ Orchestra, Band
❑ Boy Scouts, Girl Scouts
❑ Chorus
❑ Christian Campus Clubs
❑ Political Clubs
❑ Social Concern Projects

❑ Sorority/Fraternity
❑ Dormitory Offices
❑ Debate Team
❑ Auto, Motorcycle, Agricultural Mechanics
❑ Chemistry
❑ Language
❑ Art
❑ Business
❑ Science Club
❑ Chess Club
❑ Future Teachers
❑ Journalism
❑ Library
❑ Math
❑ Photography
❑ Safety Patrol
❑ School Newspaper
❑ Speech Club
❑ Yearbook Staff
❑ Building Trades
❑ Radio Broadcasting
❑ Home Economics
❑ Industrial Arts
❑ Other _____

CHURCH ACTIVITIES
❑ Missionary Benefits
❑ Evangelism
❑ Organized Social Activities
❑ Nursery
❑ Choir/Special Music/Tours
❑ Visitation
❑ Master of Ceremonies
❑ Bible Studies
❑ Youth Groups
❑ Sunday School Classes
❑ Conferences/Retreats
❑ Board Memberships
❑ Trustee
❑ Teaching Classes
❑ Special Committees
❑ Summer Programs
❑ Camp Programs
❑ Discipline
❑ Other _____

B. List other experiences you have enjoyed and work duties if applicable.

*Enjoyable Work Experiences*

_____

_____

_____

_____

*Other Experiences, Hobbies,*
*and Activities You Have Enjoyed*

_____

_____

_____

_____

C. Having jogged your memory, make a list of the top ten experiences you enjoyed most—for the sheer joy of it. Don't spend a lot of time deciding which is most enjoyable. Just write down ten of your most enjoyable experiences.

   Don't give preference to a job experience unless it was truly enjoyable. Those activities you enjoyed before becoming a Christian are as valid as those you now enjoy provided you have not lost your zest for them.

*My Ten Most Enjoyable Experiences*

1. _____

2. _____

3. _____

4. _____

5. _____

6. _____

7. _____

8. _____

9. _____

10. _____

## THE NEXT STEP

Congratulations! You're on your way to evaluating the contents of your sixth suitcase. You should now be confident that you *do* have unique experiences. These will be the key to lead us to your natural talents as they have led thousands of others.

In the next chapters, we'll help you identify these talents in three key categories of giftedness. Then in chapters 6 through 10, we'll lead you through the process of understanding how you might apply them in major areas of your life.

By the time you finish going through this book, you should be thoroughly familiar with what's in your sixth suitcase and how to take it on the road in your journey through life. Notice the special section at the end of this chapter, "Reflections for Your Journey." These study guides have been created to help you work through the personal implications of the issues you'll be coming across, consider relevant

Scripture passages, and adapt the material for group study and interaction. As you work through these questions, you'll be able to deepen, personalize, and apply the process that the following chapters will guide you through.

Once you've finished your reflections, take the next step in chapter 2 to discover your talents in the way you communicate.

## REFLECTIONS FOR YOUR JOURNEY

The questions in these special sections suggest reflections for your journey to excellence. Use them to springboard you into personal Bible study, stimulate applications of the material we've presented to you, and urge you on to take action in developing your God-given talents.

Each "Reflections" guide includes suggestions for groups who are using this book together. We hope you have made the choice to select a study group environment for working through *Discovering Your Natural Talents*. It will provide a helpful context for discussing changes in your life with others who are in a similar process. We believe that a support group offers the greatest potential for change.

If you're not involved in a group study of this material, at the very least seek out someone you can talk to about your experience in reading this book. Once you've worked through the questions in these special sections, you'll have plenty of material to discuss with a friend or mentor.

1. In this chapter you learned about six suitcases and how they accommodate people's description of themselves. What does Romans 12:3-8 teach us about how we ought to view ourselves and others?

2. What does the Bible tell us about God's plan and purpose for our lives? Consider Philippians 1:3-6, Ephesians 2:10, and any other passages you may be familiar with.

3. Consider your list of ten enjoyable experiences. Try to re-enact some of those that happened long ago. Note the enjoyment factor.

4. Describe your worst experience of burnout. What hope do you have that you need not experience this kind of burnout again?

5. What insights do these passages offer about acknowledging who we are and how God has gifted us?

Hebrews 13:5

Philippians 4:11-13

*For Group Discussion*

6. Take turns sharing at least one enjoyed experience. Try to relive it. Tell your group why it was so enjoyable.

7. Go around the group to have each person complete the sentence "I am tired of . . ." with one answer. Repeat this process four times. You might want to ask a few people to take notes of the frustrations voiced. Then reflect back on the answers as a group—discuss what was said, what was felt, patterns that may be emerging, and so on.

# TWO

# THE WAY YOU
# COMMUNICATE

eet Steve. He is forty-three, married, slightly balding, and the father of two teenagers. For twelve years Steve has worked for a Christian college. He was promoted to registrar, his current position, five years ago.

Up until ten months ago, Steve had always felt reasonably secure in this position. He did a good job and received strong performance reviews. But then his supervisor retired, and he inherited a new boss. Although there were few changes to his job duties, Steve began to sense something was wrong.

Steve's uneasiness was confirmed when he received his first performance review from his new supervisor. The report included the following surprises: Steve was "too laid back," "unresponsive," and "slow to make decisions." The final comment was: "Steve appears to be holding too high a management position for his level of ability."

Now meet Cheryl. She is eighteen, lives with her parents, and is about to graduate from high school. She is looking forward to getting her first full-time job.

One of Cheryl's primary motivations to get a job is to have her own spending money. In recent years there has been a significant tension between her taste for clothes and her parents' reluctance to fund her expanding wardrobe. But to Cheryl, clothes are more than "apparel" or simple body covering. She is extremely careful about how she dresses, sometimes changing her clothes several times a day. She shops carefully and often. "She'll have a hard time finding a job that can pay enough to support her habit," her father and mother say.

Although Cheryl argues with her parents, internally she accepts much of their doubt regarding her priorities. Not only is she afraid of being labeled a clotheshorse, she fears becoming an irresponsible adult unable to manage her finances. Unfortunately, her fears have transferred into self-doubt about her image.

## ARE WE SPEAKING THE SAME LANGUAGE?

It may not seem that Steve and Cheryl have anything in common, but they do share one basic problem. Its source is found in the way they communicate. Their communication problem is not verbal misunderstanding or lack of clarity or shyness. *Both Steve and Cheryl have natural communication strengths that are in conflict with the expectations of their superiors.*

When John evaluated Steve, he found that his key communication strengths were in writing and conversing. Steve also had a definite non-strength in giving stand-up presentations.

As you may be guessing, Steve's new boss, an accomplished college vice president, excelled at stand-up presentations. He used this favorite communication mode during staff meetings to relate information and get feedback. He also requested impromptu presentations from Steve and the other college department managers. In this system, Steve was a fish out of water. He could not "think on his feet," and so could not communicate his achievements clearly in a presentation format. Compared to other managers, he appeared weak and indecisive.

What Steve needed to do was use his natural strengths to offset his non-strengths. His natural strengths were in writing and in one-to-one conversations, so it was recommended that he arrange private sessions with his boss to talk through the progress his department was making and get a realistic view of what was expected of him.

Cheryl's problem also lay in the failure to recognize her unique communication style. When John assessed her talents, he found she had a strength in using *colors and patterns*. People with this talent often use the clothes they wear to express their feelings or thoughts. The color and texture of the clothes themselves are a message (this is also true of room decor, furniture, carpeting, drapery, and so on). To them, wearing the wrong clothes for the occasion or context would be like others walking into a formal meeting barefoot—clearly inappropriate.

A great deal of Cheryl's anxiety was resolved just by learning that she was gifted by God to express herself through *colors and patterns*. Now she knew that she wasn't a compulsive or irresponsible shopper. Although her spending was excessive, it now made sense—and so became manageable. Her parents' comments no longer threatened her. She realized that within reasonable financial limits, it was all right to be concerned about her clothes and the "message" they portrayed.

At the same time, Cheryl needed to behave more responsibly. Instead of constantly buying more clothes, she could benefit from some training in color coordination that would enable her to be more selective. Understanding her natural *communication* strength allowed her to accept herself. Instead of being some kind of freak, she was a talented person seeking expression. This also helped her select a career goal that paid her to be expressive with *colors and patterns* (interior design, textile design, home remodeling).

The kind of communication problem that Steve and Cheryl experienced is usually behind statements such as, "He's a little strange at first, but after you get to know him he's okay." Or, "She seemed like an airhead, but then I found out she really has a lot on the ball."

Look past the apparent harshness of these comments to consider what is going on. Sometimes people appear not to say anything worthwhile, but if they are allowed to express themselves in their natural mode, they make a valuable contribution. You too can make a valuable contribution. Grasp this important truth:

> *You have at least one predominant capacity for communicating your thoughts, ideas, and feelings.*

In this chapter we'll be examining three major areas of communication aptitude: verbal, artistic, and performing. Then we'll help you discover which aptitude you may possess in one, two, or all three of these areas.

## VERBAL COMMUNICATION TALENTS

Verbal strengths are usually demonstrated in one or more of the following areas:

*1. Writing Words*
*The ability to communicate thoughts, feelings, and ideas clearly in written form.* This may take varying forms, whether in business reports, personal diaries, creative writing, journalism, or correspondence. The person with this strength might enjoy writing letters rather than making telephone calls.

### 2. Conversing
*The ability to interact skillfully and enjoyably in conversation.* Here are those who enjoy and excel at interpersonal discussion with mutual give-and-take and understanding.

### 3. Public Speaking (or Preaching)
*The ability to stand before a group and present information persuasively and clearly to an audience.* This talent usually favors presenting one's opinion to obtain some type of audience response. It does not favor audience give-and-take dialogue. (See Talent 15, "Giving Presentations.") A person who is strong in this area can get and hold the audience's attention, increasing their receptiveness to the message. Something in natural speakers seems to come alive when they get in front of a group.

### 4. Teaching
*The ability to present information in a way that enhances understanding as opposed to presenting one's view.* As in public speaking, this skill involves presenting information clearly (here, to a group or an individual). But while speaking focuses on emotion, persuasion, and application, the teaching talent focuses on deepening understanding and stimulating critical thinking.

### 5. Broadcasting
*The use of any electronic media—including radio, television, tapes, or telephone—to present information.* The telephone is the most readily available tool, so strength in this area usually is revealed here first. Those with broadcasting talent enjoy using the phone; those without this strength appreciate its convenience but often feel it is too limiting.

## ARTISTIC COMMUNICATION TALENTS

Artistic strengths show themselves in people who communicate primarily in these areas:

### 6. Designing
*The ability to convey inner thoughts and feelings through graphic media.* This includes a wide spectrum of the arts. It could manifest itself in areas such as commercial design, theater set design, drawing and painting, computer graphics, or technical illustration.

### 7. Painting
The painting talent expresses more than a picture; color and texture are part of the communication.

### 8. Using Colors and Patterns
*The ability to communicate mood or shape environment through use of color, texture, and pattern.* This was Cheryl's talent. She used clothes to express herself. Others who are talented in this area might pursue interior design, photography, textile design, even cake decorating.

### 9. Using Shapes and Forms
*The talent for communicating through defining interior space and manipulation of raw materials and finished objects.* This talent uses the arrangement of forms and shapes in areas such as sculpture, landscaping, or interior furniture arrangement.

### 10. Using Handicrafts
*The ability to use hand tools to create finished products out of materials such as wood, leather, cloth, and yarn.* Skills here include needlepoint, knitting, tile painting, woodcarving, etc. Most people have dabbled in this area, but those with a strength usually make it an enjoyable prolonged activity.

### 11. Composing Music
*The ability to convey feeling and thought through composing, arranging, or directing music.* Artistic skill in music involves creating and/or producing it rather than simply performing it.

## PERFORMING COMMUNICATION TALENTS

Talent in performance-related communication manifests itself in these areas:

### 12. Acting
*The talent that excels at projecting a mood or feeling or recreating a character type by changing one's external countenance, behavior, or personality type.* Many kindergarten teachers, speakers, and politicians have this strength. Surprisingly, this is the key talent for cross-cultural ministry, because it enables a person to adjust quickly to a new lifestyle and daily habit.

### 13. Moderating
*The talent of facilitating discussion among a group of people.* Many people noted for their instructional ability use moderating as a primary method of communication because they can draw responses out of their students. Individuals with this strength are quick to discern and articulate various positions and how they relate to each other.

### 14. Musical Performance
*The ability to perform musically, alone or in front of a group.* This includes both singing and playing an instrument. People who display this talent often become "a different person" during their performances. It is amazing how many times a person can get up in front of a church, sing, capture the hearts of the congregation, then sit down without saying a word. This person, seated quietly, gives no clue to the dynamic energy released by musical performance.

### 15. Giving Presentations
*The ability to communicate information, guide a meeting, or elicit a response while in front of an audience.* This is the natural talent that enables a person to make announcements

or lead a meeting or service with give-and-take audience participation. Seminar and workshop presentations with audience give and take are a favorite in this area. Performance here usually requires no rehearsal. This area was a non-strength for Steve.

## HOW TO DISTINGUISH
## YOUR WISHES FROM YOUR REALITY

While reading this list you probably identified with some of the explanations and started thinking, "Ah, this is my *communication* strength." Chances are good that you're right.

However, be on guard against making premature conclusions. Throughout your lifetime you have been subject to many influences that may have encouraged you to build with a *communication* strength that you don't have, or neglect the talents that are uniquely yours. When this happens, you may find that you are attempting construction of another bridge over the Grand Canyon. The issue is not what you can do well but where God has gifted you to be the best.

Consider the case of Denise, who came to John as a twenty-year-old college sophomore. She was so frustrated with where she was heading that she was practically despondent.

Denise was a music major, working toward her bachelor's degree. When she completed the Talent Discovery Guide, she discovered that she was not as gifted in music as other *communication* talents. Quite a problem for a music major!

Construction on Denise's air bridge had begun when she was quite young, with the help of her parents, both professional musicians. Since music was highly esteemed in her home, and because young Denise was anxious to please her parents (like most youngsters), she began to play the piano. With two built-in tutors, she quickly acquired playing skills. Her parents praised her accomplishments.

Her teachers at school told her, "You're a gifted musician."

Unfortunately, neither Denise's parents nor her teachers distinguished between motivated skill and natural talent. Denise had technical skill, but she did not have a top *communication* strength in music. She was what musicians call a "mechanical" musician.

It wouldn't be fair to fault Denise's parents and teachers for encouraging her to continue in music, nor Denise for assuming that she should pursue a vocation in music. But this conditioning process helped produce an unrealistic ambition.

After Denise learned that her true *communication* strengths were in *writing* and using *colors and patterns*, she changed her major to media production (video and motion picture) and began a much happier and healthier future.

Like Denise, Cheryl, and Steve, you too can benefit from the discovery of your *communication* strength: For them it helped self-image, interpersonal relations, career choice, job security, and family harmony. Even if you aren't facing difficulties in these areas, you will benefit by learning to express yourself in your unique way. You will begin turning mediocrity into excellence.

True self-expression is important because most people hold on to their first impression of you. If you don't have the opportunity to show your dominant *communication* strength in a credible way, people may dismiss your ability to make worthwhile contributions. Right or wrong, your communication is regarded as a banner signifying your worth, value, and significance.

The perception of your value is often established by teachers, employers, or church boards who have preconceived notions about *communication* strengths. Unfortunately, some people tend to assume that others ought to use a particular mode of communication. Their faulty assumption is that you should be just as capable as they are in that communication style.

## A PICTURE CAN BE WORTH A THOUSAND WORDS

This same line of reasoning often assumes that artistic communication is not as important as verbal communication, and so therefore art and music are not important channels of communication. People who make this assumption usually feel that nobody understands what artists are "saying" anyway.

In contrast to this faulty thinking is a musician we heard about who composed and recorded a musical piece for the hammer dulcimer that reflected his feelings after a close friend died in an automobile accident. Though the title of the song does not reveal the subject matter, he has received several letters from people telling him that it was a comfort to them after a dear one died.

Many of those with artistic strengths will go to a gallery and spend a long time gazing at various works of art. Interviews with these people have revealed that many times they feel they are carrying on a conversation with the artist by looking at the painting or sculpture. Moods and motion are conveyed through the colors, design, and the "sense" of the art.

The strengths of artistically talented people are sometimes the cause of school achievement problems. There is a strong tendency among educators to value word skills and speaking ability higher than other *communication* strengths. Therefore, people adept at speaking or writing usually do well in school. The good grades they receive, based largely on their verbal skills, develop their self-confidence.

Conversely, the talent of craftsmen, artists, or actors who express themselves through their art form is often devalued in school because word skills are considered more important. Consequently, these individuals have a more difficult time gaining positive recognition. This pall can hang on for the rest of their lives.

Not all problems are rooted in the emphasis on verbal

communication. And after all, there are only so many ways to say, "Please pass the pepper." But you might be surprised by how big a role nonverbal communication plays in our lives.

For example, how do you say, "I love you"? Do you: Draw a picture? Make a greeting card? Compose or sing a song? Bake cookies? Carve a woodcut? Sew an article of clothing? Send flowers? Smile?

All these love messages are nonverbal. In a day when so much emphasis has been placed upon verbal skills, it is interesting to note the popularity of Pictionary, a game that uses drawing to communicate. Perhaps this talent has been bottled up and is now free to express itself.

Nonverbal communication can be very important in a business context. The most successful restaurants, hotels, convention centers, and resorts usually have an environment that makes their patrons feel relaxed, comfortable, and at ease. Restaurant owners know the saying, "People eat with their eyes." This refers not only to appearance of food on the plate, but also to the tablecloth, napkins, flowers, carpet, room decor and everything else in the immediate environment. Many of us tend to choose restaurants as much for atmosphere as for food.

## DISCOVERING THE WAY YOU COMMUNICATE

God has created a multitude of methods of expression—talking, writing, performing, acting, drawing, crafting, and decorating are but a few we have looked at. He intended them to be used like instruments in an orchestra: none to dominate, all to contribute. He loves us all equally, and He loves all forms of expression equally. Only people with a distorted perspective label some abilities "better" or "worse" than others.

So often in ministry contexts we have noticed that the expression of *public speaking* (or *preaching*) is elevated above other forms of expression. In God's sight *public speaking* is no more important than *graphic designing.*

God's orchestra needs us all. Trumpets are not more important than woodwinds; they're just louder.

Now it's time to discover which instrument you play best in this orchestra. Your natural way of communicating is likely to be the mode you find easiest and most enjoyable. It very likely showed up often in the list of "My Ten Most Enjoyable Experiences" you filled out in chapter 1.

## THE TALENT DISCOVERY GUIDE—
## COMMUNICATION

Write your ten most enjoyable experiences from your list in chapter 1 in the vertical lines of the chart below. "Softball" is written in as an example.

Then, starting with the first *communication* talent, "writing," determine if your experience allowed you to demonstrate that talent. If you generally use that ability, put a check mark opposite it as in the "softball" example.

When you're finished marking the *communication* talents you used in your first experience, mark each of your other nine experiences. Then count the number of check marks across each horizontal line corresponding to a given talent. In the right-hand column under "Total," write in the number of check marks on that line.

| | Softball | 1 | 2 | 3 | 4 | 5 | 6 | 7 | 8 | 9 | 10 | TOTAL |
|---|---|---|---|---|---|---|---|---|---|---|---|---|
| **I. CONCERNING COMMUNICATION** (at least one best capacity) | | | | | | | | | | | | ███ |
| A. USING WORDS | | | | | | | | | | | | |
| **1. Writing Words** Writing clearly understood reports, letters, essays, stories, scripts, advertisements, contracts, curricula, magazine articles, and the like. | | | | | | | | | | | | |
| **2. Conversing** Talking one on one, sharing ideas and feelings, discussing current events, exchanging views, explaining things with a high degree of mutual understanding. | ✔ | | | | | | | | | | | |
| **3. Speaking in Public** Communicating clearly and persuasively to a *live* audience, such as a committee, club, church congregation, or other gathering, with limited audience interaction. | | | | | | | | | | | | |
| **4. Teaching** Helping others fully understand a subject, topic, or idea in a classroom, seminar, workshop, club, association, church, or other group setting. | ✔ | | | | | | | | | | | |
| **5. Broadcasting** Communicating clearly through electronic media such as video, radio, telephone, or audio cassette recording. | | | | | | | | | | | | |
| B. BEING ARTISTIC | | | | | | | | | | | | |
| **6. Designing** Sketches, illustrations, graphic arts, theater set designs, murals, or other design projects. | | | | | | | | | | | | |

| | Softball | 1 | 2 | 3 | 4 | 5 | 6 | 7 | 8 | 9 | 10 | TOTAL |
|---|---|---|---|---|---|---|---|---|---|---|---|---|
| **7. Painting**<br>With oils, pastels, watercolors, and chalk. | | | | | | | | | | | | |
| **8. Using Colors and Patterns**<br>Expressing my thoughts or feelings through colors or patterns as in interior decor, clothing, makeup, jewelry, house-painting, and the like. | | | | | | | | | | | | |
| **9. Using Shapes and Forms**<br>Expressing my thoughts or feelings through shaping forms as in sculpturing, architectural designing, landscaping, furniture arranging, or the like. | | | | | | | | | | | | |
| **10. Using Handicrafts**<br>Projecting my thoughts or feelings through handcrafted items made of wood, leather, cloth, plastic, and the like. | | | | | | | | | | | | |
| **11. Composing Music**<br>Expressing my thoughts or feelings by writing, composing, or arranging works of music. | | | | | | | | | | | | |
| **C. PERFORMING** | | | | | | | | | | | | |
| **12. Acting**<br>Expressing a mood or feeling through role playing, acting, telling jokes, doing character impersonations or mime in either informal conversation or theatrical settings. | | | | | | | | | | | | |
| **13. Moderating**<br>Guiding a group discussion, hosting a panel presentation, or coordinating discussion between people or groups. | ✔ | | | | | | | | | | | |

| | Softball | 1 | 2 | 3 | 4 | 5 | 6 | 7 | 8 | 9 | 10 | TOTAL |
|---|---|---|---|---|---|---|---|---|---|---|---|---|
| **14. Singing or Instrument Performing** Singing or playing an instrument in front of others as part of an orchestra, choir, ensemble, duet, band, or as a soloist. | | | | | | | | | | | | |
| **15. Giving Presentations** Giving presentations in front of others, such as in sales presentations, question-answer workshops, announcements, selected readings, and product service demonstrations. | | | | | | | | | | | | |

Now review your total scores in the far-right column. Select one to three talents that you feel best describe your most effective *communication* talents. Circle them on the chart.

## THE NEXT STEP

We hope you're beginning to feel encouraged by how easy—although time-consuming—it is to discover how God has gifted you. You've now taken the first two steps through the Talent Discovery Guide, a portion of which appears in chapters 1 through 4.

Understanding your strengths in *communication* is crucial to the rest of your discovery process. You'll be building on this understanding as we move into the next chapter and explore the way you relate.

## REFLECTIONS FOR YOUR JOURNEY

1. What appear to be the *communication* strengths of the following people as revealed in these passages?

Paul—Acts 14:12

Luke—Acts 1:1-2

Dorcas—Acts 9:36, 39

2. a. What nonverbal expressions did David use to express his inner joy? (2 Samuel 6:14-16, Psalm 149:3)

b. What *communication* talent(s) do you think these expressions represent?

3. a. David also authored seventy-three psalms. What *communication* talent(s) do you think this reveals?

b. Today many psalms have been set to music and song. How does this change the communication process? How is hearing God's Word in a contemporary song different from reading God's Word?

4. In some cases a person's primary talent strength has not been fully developed or used. It is a "raw" talent, like gold still in the ground. How would you suggest a person who thinks he or she has an undeveloped talent verify this conclusion?

5. a. How are you currently using your *communication* strengths?

   b. Can you think of ways to use them more effectively? Write down any thoughts you have.

6. a. What (if any) responsibilities do you have at home, work, or church that require you to use one of your communication *non*-strengths?

b. Think about your level of performance in this non-strength area. Are you doing an adequate job in this responsibility? If not, how might you improve your proficiency in this responsibility?

*For Group Discussion*

7. Take turns telling each other your top *communication* talent(s). As each person shares this evaluation, group members should verify the conclusions by mentioning examples they've noticed of how this person demonstrates those talents.

8. If any members are unsure of their *communication* talents, ask the group to provide suggestions for helping them to identify and begin to use their strengths.

# THREE

# THE WAY YOU RELATE

hree adjectives often used to describe Bill were genuine, enthusiastic, and goal-oriented. That's why many people thought of him as a salesman. "You could sell ice to an Eskimo," they would say.

Bill took this in and thought, *You know, I bet I could sell ice to an Eskimo if I learned how.* So Bill read books and learned sales techniques and went out to be a good salesman.

He had some initial success, but not enough to be financially comfortable. He drove himself harder, read more, and worked on positive thinking, time management, and communication skills. He tried to keep his enthusiasm high, but he began to feel that he was dragging a dead weight behind him when he went out to sell.

Bill began to hate his prospect lists, the telephone that

he used to make appointments, and most of all going out and visiting prospective customers. So finally, he quit.

Sometime later Bill entered "full-time Christian ministry." He was excited about being involved with something that had an important purpose. No longer would he have to sell something in order to make a dollar. He was working to help people change their lives and follow Jesus Christ. This significance gave him a new enthusiasm for his work.

But within just a few weeks of involvement in this new vocation, Bill began to experience the same frustration he had when he was a salesman.

## DIFFERENT STROKES FOR DIFFERENT FOLKS

It wasn't hard to figure out why Bill experienced the same frustration—he was functioning the same way he did when he was a salesman. He was visiting pastors and other church leaders and explaining the ministry in which he was involved. He did not consider himself to be a salesman in this new position, however, because he had no quotas to fulfill and his salary did not depend upon results. But in fact, he was doing the same kind of new people contact work that he had done as a salesman.

What was the common source of Bill's frustration? *The way he related to people.* Bill's *relational* talent did not fit well in a multiple-new-people environment. So every time he tried, he was exerting excessive energy. Neither his desire to make money nor his more noble desire to serve God were sufficient motivation for him to maintain these activities for an extended period of time. The stress was too much.

Curiously enough, the same three adjectives—genuine, enthusiastic, and goal-oriented—were used to described Bill's adult daughter Carolyn. But no one ever suggested that she become a salesperson. Because of stereotypical thinking about vocational directions for women, people envisioned her in a different slot altogether.

But after Carolyn completed college, she took a job at a jewelry store that was part of a national chain. Within weeks, she became the top salesperson in the store, and within a year she won two sales awards in her district. She found selling easy, natural, and rewarding.

Carolyn functioned very well in a multiple-new-people environment. Her father, on the other hand, functioned best when he interacted with a smaller number of people whom he had gotten to know over a period of time. Bill and Carolyn had personality traits in common, but their talent differences in relating to people were the key factor in whether a sales position was frustrating or rewarding.

We use three categories to describe how God has gifted us in relating to others:

*16. Multi-Relational*
*Establishing rapport with new people quickly and easily upon first encounter.* Usually capable of maintaining multiple relationships over an extended period of time.

*17. Familiar Group Relational*
*Establishing rapport with people after repeated meetings.* Enjoys joint work projects, department meetings, or group sessions. Usually capable of strengthening and sustaining group membership.

*18. Singular Relational*
*Establishing rapport with people after long-term contact.* Highly capable of working on extended projects by oneself.

## RELATING TO OTHERS

*Familiar group* people are excellent team players and enjoy accomplishing common goals together. But a woodcarver *(singular relational)* doesn't need anyone to help him or her make a product. And a public relations specialist *(multi-*

*relational)* has to have a lot of people around to function. Both the woodcarver and the public relations person can be team players, but they probably will function more like a track team than a volleyball team.

We find that based upon our counseling experience, study, and research, approximately 15 percent of the population is *multi-relational,* 70 percent is *familiar group relational,* and another 15 percent is *singular relational.* Most people will have *one* dominant talent.

These categories help explain why most people are at their best in small group Bible studies and Sunday school classes (*familiar group* activities) and are less enthusiastic about studying their lesson at home (*singular relational* activity) or doing door-to-door evangelism (*multi-relational* activity).

We're not advocating that each of us stick to just those spiritual activities that are tailored to our relational preference. The Christian faith often calls us to responsibilities in areas that make us uncomfortable or in which we are not personally strong. But we will function best and enjoy life most if we spend the bulk of our time (60 percent) interacting with people in our area of natural strength.

These *relational* strength groupings do not have hard and fast boundaries. Think of them as on a continuum, going from one extreme of very *singular* to the other extreme of very *multi-relational.* You may be *familiar group relational,* but tend either to the *singular* or to the *multi-relational.*

## THE NEED FOR FREEDOM

Those who are oriented toward the far right or left of this continuum of *relational* strengths are outnumbered, and therefore may sometimes feel like outsiders. *Singular relational* people, for example, often feel guilty about their desire to work alone or about maintaining fewer relationships. They may feel pressured by the assumption that loving others means relating to a lot of people, or that they should be cultivating many friends and continually inviting them to church.

This pressure from unrealistic and mistaken assumptions can be increased by the charge that *singular relational* people are "antisocial." This unfair and insensitive criticism overlooks the reality that there are natural differences in how we relate to others. It also does not stop to consider that the gifted *singular relational* person may have as great an impact on others through deeper and more long-lasting friendships with a few people.

Let's illustrate this problem of misunderstanding. A church will often be more favorable toward a new candidating pastor who is *multi-relational* oriented. They quickly feel the warmth and relational energy that this talent displays. The process of candidating (unfortunately) reinforces this discrimination by being preferential to *multi-relational* people. The prospective pastor comes for a few days, delivers a sermon, and meets a wide variety of many new people. (Note that most scholars tend to be *singular relational*.)

Since it is easy for *multi-relational* individuals to develop new relationships, they are selected more often than people with other strengths. Once they're in place, they naturally expect everyone to follow their example. But only 15 percent of the population is *multi-relational*. That would force 85 percent to fabricate a *multi-relational* strength—producing an unnatural stress God does not intend. Dale Carnegie's book *How To Win Friends and Influence People* has been popular because most people don't naturally do what wins friends quickly.

We want to reinforce the validity of *familiar group* and *singular relational* lifestyles, in addition to affirming *multi-relational* methodologies. Let's stop holding each other to arbitrary standards of performance, Christian or otherwise, and work toward an atmosphere of acceptance and encouragement—each of us excelling in our areas of God-given strength and achieving basic adequacy in areas of biblical responsibility where we are not strong. Let's give each other the freedom to operate out of our unique strengths. If God has chosen not to create "well-rounded" relational talented people, let's not burn out ourselves and others trying to do it all.

There are many applications in life for your *relational* strength. Consider the conflicts in social life that can result in a marriage when husband and wife have different relational talents. Relational talents also affect your job, your so-called success in school, your church, your friendships, and just about every other area of life.

## RELATIONAL STRENGTHS
## AND EVANGELISM STRATEGIES

Consider the application of this understanding of *relational* strengths to a key area of the Christian life: witnessing and evangelism. Perhaps seeing how this concept applies to this area will help you apply it to other areas.

Many of the evangelism models we've all been encouraged to follow involve *multi-relational* people who led someone to Christ after only a brief encounter. For the 85 percent who are not *multi-relational,* this model sets up a stress-producing or unnatural standard. They may try for a while to follow this example, but in the long haul they will drop it because it demands too much personal energy.

In recent years, a wave of books and strategies has advocated what is commonly called friendship evangelism. The concept is to become a caring friend to those you wish to lead to Christ, instead of simply confronting them with a gospel presentation as your initial, and sometimes final, contact. It is easy to see why this approach has become very popular. Most people (70 percent) have familiar group *relational* strengths, which are of primary importance in this evangelistic strategy.

The problem of imposing a *multi-relational* evangelism strategy across the board is even more marked when it is forced on those with *singular relational* strengths. *Singular relational* people are at their best with their closest friends and when people come to them and ask questions. If they are forced to initiate many relationships, and artificially speed up the relational process to get to spiritual issues quickly, they are bound to suffer stress.

Evangelism strategies that include *singular relational* people could include counseling with those who have already been "warmed up," such as referrals from a pastor and people who show interest at crusades or retreats—in sharp contrast to door-to-door confrontations.

We hope these thoughts begin to free you from narrow thinking about sharing your faith. As we focus on God working through each of us according to His plan, using our natural talents, we can be free from guilt and fruitful in evangelism.

## DISCOVERING THE WAY YOU RELATE

Although each day you are faced with challenges to interact with people at many different levels, you have one best mode of how you consistently relate to others. Identifying your *relational* strength will help you focus your expectations regarding your personal interaction with others. You'll find your confidence increasing and your defensiveness decreasing as you build on your strengths without need to apologize for areas of non-strength.

### THE TALENT DISCOVERY GUIDE—RELATIONSHIPS

As in the previous chapter, list the same ten most enjoyable experiences in the vertical columns. Then put check marks in the columns that correspond to demonstrated talents. Put your total in the far-right column. As in the previous chart, "Softball" is given as an example.

| | Softball | 1 | 2 | 3 | 4 | 5 | 6 | 7 | 8 | 9 | 10 | TOTAL |
|---|---|---|---|---|---|---|---|---|---|---|---|---|
| **II. CONCERNING RELATIONSHIPS** (one best capacity) | | | | | | | | | | | | |
| **16. Multi-Relational** Preferring to meet new people as well as being with people I already know. | | | | | | | | | | | | |
| **17. Familiar Group Relational** Preferring to be with people I already know. Also willing to meet new people or work on a task by myself. | ✔ | | | | | | | | | | | |
| **18. Singular Relational** Preferring to be by myself, working on a project. Also willing to be with people I know well. | | | | | | | | | | | | |

Review your total scores for your *relational* talents. Select the one you feel best describes your *relational* strength, and circle it on the chart.

## THE NEXT STEP

You're halfway through exploring the contents of your sixth suitcase. Armed with a good working knowledge of how you communicate and how you relate, you're now ready to explore your best ways of performing tasks and completing activities—the way you function.

## REFLECTIONS FOR YOUR JOURNEY

1. a. Each of the passages below records incidents in which Jesus related to others. Characterize the nature

of Jesus' *relational* aptitude in each of these occurrences by marking "M," "F," or "S" indicating *multi-relational, familiar group relational,* or *singular relational.* (Note: To the best of our knowledge, only Jesus has a strength in all three *relational* areas.)

Matthew 4:23-25 _____
John 11:5 _____
John 13:1-5 _____
John 17:25 _____

b. How do these passages provide insights into the description of Jesus in Hebrews 2:17-18?



2. What *relational* talent was demonstrated by the Twelve in Acts 6:1-6?


3. a. What does Romans 15:7 teach about how we should act toward those who have a different *relational* talent than ours?



b. When, if ever, have you had a hard time fulfilling this command?

4. How do you think the teaching of 1 Corinthians 12:21-26 should be applied to the variety of *relational* talents?

5. List one important contribution per *relational* strength that can be made in your congregation. If possible, note a specific example of each.

Multi-Relational Contribution

Familiar Group Relational Contribution

Singular Relational Contribution

6. Most people (approximately 70 percent) are *familiar group relational.*

a. If you are in either of the other two categories, write down your memory of any time that you felt like an oddball. If you are *multi-relational,* record any feelings about people who are critical or "hold back."

b. If you are *familiar group relational,* what do you think you can do to help prevent *multi-relational* and *singular relational* people from feeling like oddballs?

*For Group Discussion*

7. Share with each other your *relational* strength. Explain how you have used it well or how you have been troubled with it.

8. Ask each other to cite examples of contemporary people with your *relational* strength who have been successful in evangelism. Discuss together ideas for following the examples of these people.

9. Brainstorm ideas for church socials that would be appealing to people in each of the three *relational* strength categories.

# FOUR

# THE WAY YOU FUNCTION

eorge, Sarah, Bob, and Ann are discussing the agenda for their couples' weekend retreat. They all agree that getting away together will help build a sense of unity among the older couples and the growing number of newcomers.

George emphatically suggests a series of recreational and athletic activities that will get everyone involved in competitive teams. He also suggests planning "quieter activities" such as bicycling, canoeing, and hiking.

Bob urges that they select a location and establish a schedule before they talk about anything else. His foremost concern is figuring the cost of the retreat up front to make sure they can even afford it.

Ann proposes bringing in a resource expert who can speak on "Coping with Stress" and follow it up with small discussion groups. "It will enable us to spend time helping each other so everyone will get the reassurance and support they need to meet their needs." She also makes a strong case for plenty of free time to take walks and enjoy the retreat setting.

Sarah advocates planning a lot of group activities—charades, board games, a slide show, group singing. "Let's give people an opportunity to be creative, to use their imagination, and to step out on new ground."

Who do you think lettered in four sports in high school?

Who do you think is an accountant and enjoys planning details?

Who do you think is usually available to friends to discuss their frustrations and problems?

Who do you think avoids the routine and likes to try new and different ideas?

## THE ROLE OF FUNCTIONAL TALENTS

Most people do not realize how much their *functional* talents impact their work preferences and judgments in life. George, who has always had strong abilities in activities requiring physical coordination, likes doing things he is good at—and assumes others will too. Bob is an accountant, and so for him financial and organizational concerns must be addressed before interpersonal issues can be discussed. Ann is a natural comforter of others and so wants to provide an encouraging and receptive environment. Sarah, creative by nature, tends to perceive structured schedules as confining. She prefers spontaneity and surprise.

All four have an individual bias that reflects their natural talents in the way they *function*. These strengths are God-given, task-oriented behavioral aptitudes that give us the capacity to perform duties and activities at remarkably high levels of excellence.

Failure to appreciate the variety of *functional* talents can cause conflict. Desire to function just as well as others can cause stress. Pursuing a strength in *functional* talents one does not naturally possess can cause burnout. However, the proper orchestration of *functional* talents can bring harmony among people and tasks.

Later in this chapter you'll be looking back at your experiences to identify which *functional* talents you used most often. But first, read carefully through the following descriptions of these thirty-six *functional* talents, which are grouped in thirteen categories.

## ORGANIZING PERSONAL TIME AND SPACE

These talents involve the effective and efficient use of one's time and space.

### 19. Organizing Time
Enables one to schedule effectively, set priorities, evaluate timing, and recognize efficiency. This talent deals with personal time organization, and differs from *planning*, which maps out activities for others.

### 20. Organizing Personal Space
Ordering and maintaining your closet, desk, work space, automobile, or any other area. Obviously, people with this talent are "neat." But not all neat people have this talent. Some keep the appearance of neatness but are not well organized, such as the person who clears off the top of the dresser by shoving everything into a drawer.

## BEING CREATIVE

This group of abilities describes the formation of new associations with previously unrelated concepts, objects, or thoughts.

### 21. Creating
Forming new ideas for systems, concepts, methods, routines, or other notions for concrete issues.

*22. Imagining*
Originating ideas for stories, theories, or other abstract concepts.

*23. Inventing*
Originating new mechanical, electrical, electronic, chemical, or other physical devices.

## SUPERVISING OTHERS

This group includes talents in directing the behavior and activities of others. (Note: Supervisory talents, which are often misunderstood, are the foundation of many air bridges. We'll be looking at these abilities in greater detail in chapter 5.)

*24. Initiating/Developing*
Coordinating the activities of others to start new programs, systems, or projects.

*25. Planning*
Establishing the long-range logistical details necessary to complete a project with consideration for time, costs, equipment, personnel, facilities, etc. Included here is scheduling the activities of others to reach goals.

*26. Managing*
Coordinating the ongoing activities or tasks of others to harmonize their efforts.

## USING BODY, HANDS, OR FINGERS

This group of talents describes four different types of body-motor coordination.

*27. Physical Coordination*
Efficient use of arms, legs, and the rest of the body for physical activity such as sports, recreation, acrobatics, ballet, etc.

### 28. Hand-Arm Coordination
Physical agility for effective use of tools in repairing, assembling, or adjusting. It is necessary for mechanics, carpenters, and plumbers.

### 29. Operating Coordination
Enables one to drive a vehicle, type, fly an airplane, manipulate heavy equipment, or operate an industrial machine.

### 30. Hand-Finger Coordination
The manual dexterity required in the use of precision instruments, such as in drafting, soldering, or model building. It is important for dentists, surgeons, watchmakers, artisans (tole painters), and many forms of electronic device repair.

## HELPING OTHERS

This group of talents can be described as a natural availability to meet the needs of others. People with these talents usually focus more on people than objectives.

### 31. Tutoring
Assisting others to overcome or cope with disabilities or learning problems. Special education teachers, social workers, and those who help the disabled may have this talent.

### 32. Being of Service
Availability to assist others with their projects, needs, or programs.

### 33. Counseling
Evaluating the emotional needs or problems of others and then helping them with suggestions, advice, or direction.

### 34. Reassuring and Supporting
Identifying with another's hurts, frustrations, or anxieties and giving comfort and emotional support.

## USING INTUITION

This is the ability to evaluate one's surroundings without the conscious use of reasoning. No one's intuition is right all the time, but those with talents in this category are right often enough to rely upon their "senses."

### 35. Evaluating People's Character
The ability to quickly and accurately discern and assess the motives of other people.

### 36. Making Future Projections
Forecasting (foreseeing) future developments in personal or public circles—trends, fads, opinion, and so on.

## BEING PERSUASIVE

These talents enable one to direct others to a course of action, a change of mood, or a commitment to follow.

### 37. Negotiating
Working out an agreement suitable to two or more parties.

### 38. Selling
The introduction of a product or idea, resulting in a purchase (also applies to recruiting volunteers). Traditionally, salesmen have been characterized negatively, but there is a legitimate place for honest salespeople.

### 39. Promoting
Motivating others to accept a new or different viewpoint, product, or program.

## OBSERVING DETAILS

These talents involve visual attention to fine points.

### 40. Physical Environment
Seeing particulars that are often overlooked, both indoors and outdoors.

### 41. Printed Documents
Observing details in written or printed matter, such as maps, blueprints, contracts, and manuscripts. Proofreaders need to notice printed details. Machinists often need to see blueprint details.

### 42. Spatial Perception
The ability to see a three-dimensional structure or object by looking at a two-dimensional design. This includes people who can follow plans for building or make objects based on drawings.

## USING NUMBERS

These talents enable one to quickly use figures readily and accurately.

### 43. Calculating
Performing numerical computation quickly and accurately.

### 44. Recording and Auditing
Accurately counting, taking inventory, or keeping numerical records.

## PROBLEM SOLVING PROCEDURES

The ability to discover the source of failure, breakdown, or error.

### 45. Troubleshooting
The ability to diagnose the cause of problems in mechanical, electrical, chemical, or other technical areas.

### 46. Problem Solving
The ability to diagnose errors in human logic, administrative procedures, or interpersonal relationships.

*Note:* Don't confuse *problem solving* or *troubleshooting* with *analyzing*, which is one of the talents in the reasoning/contemplating category. An *analyzing* talent creates a quest for knowledge of why things are the way they are; a *problem solving* talent assesses why something is not the way it's supposed to be, trying to get to the root cause.

## HANDLING INFORMATION

The ability to deal with facts, data, and other types of raw information.

### 47. Researching/Investigating
Seeking and gathering pertinent information, including records, archives, and genealogies, etc.

### 48. Remembering
The ability to quickly recall data such as names, dates, locations, events, qualities, etc.

### 49. Classifying
The efficient and orderly arrangement of information to make it more accessible and therefore useful.

## REASONING/CONTEMPLATING

These talents focus on the mental processing of information.

### 50. Analyzing
Examining an object or idea in order to understand it. In this process one continually asks, "Why?"—such as in questioning the phenomenon of photosynthesis or the nature of the universe. This is usually an academic talent closely tied to scholarship. It closely resembles the quest to know discussed in Proverbs.

### 51. Appraising/Evaluating

Estimating the value or feasibility of a new product, business venture, investment, or program—especially in order to project future outcome or financial return. People with this strength are to be consulted.

### 52. Synthesizing

Combining previously unrelated ideas or data in some cohesive manner, usually while retaining the individual identities of the parts.

## MAKING DECISIONS

The ability to act instinctively with limited information by being decisive or by taking risks, especially in an emergency situation.

### 53. Being Decisive

Quickly and correctly responding to a problem, emergency, or unexpected situation—such as in medical emergencies, military warfare, live broadcasting programs, or sports.

### 54. Taking Risks

The capacity to make decisions in situations in which the odds of possible gain or loss are fifty-fifty—often in business ventures, investing, or trying something new.

## DISCOVERING THE WAY YOU FUNCTION

Among these thirty-six functional talents, you have at least three to five strengths. We want you to claim your strengths and develop them. We also want you to accept the fact that others have strengths that are different from yours.

You also have some non-strengths—at least three to five *functional* non-strengths in addition to *relational* and *communication* ones. These are God-given limitations, even though they may fall in areas that are vital to your family, job, or lifestyle. By acknowledging your non-strengths instead of trying to hide or ignore them, you can open yourself to interdependent relationships rather than forcing yourself into a competitive, defensive, or independent lifestyle.

Interdependence blends people whose strengths are different. We've discovered that some *functional* talents are opposites—the abilities seem to be mutually exclusive of each other. After much study, research, and many thousands of assessments and interviews, we have found certain talents that are polarized. It may help you to identify where you think you belong in the following sets of opposites.

The first pair of opposites contrasts the categories of *organizing personal space* versus *being creative*. Those who are best at maintaining order, regularity, and routine are usually not extremely creative. Orderly people deal with *what is* rather than with *what could be*. On the other hand, those who are creative generally don't maintain structure well. They tend to experiment with new possibilities rather than maintain policies, rules, and regulations. Creative people may challenge the standards to try it a different way.

The second pair of mutually exclusive talents includes the categories of *helping others* and *supervising others*. Those with helping talents appear to wait for something to happen and then provide comfort and support. They respond to obvious individual need by encouraging and comforting. The *supervisory* talents, by contrast, make things happen. They see the big picture, set direction, challenge, confront, and charge ahead. They point the way for others to follow.

People with either of these talent "opposites" should use their strength and accept their limitation (the opposite talent). However, they should not excuse themselves from attaining a level of adequacy in the opposing talent. Your creativity doesn't give you license to be totally disorganized. Your *supervisory* strengths don't give you the right to railroad others into accepting your ideas. (More about *supervisory* talents in the next chapter.)

## THE TALENT DISCOVERY GUIDE—
## FUNCTIONAL CAPACITIES

By now you should be familiar with the format of the Talent Discovery Guide. To identify your *functional* talents, complete the exercise below for each of your ten enjoyable experiences. After you complete this exercise, you'll identify your top three to five *functional* strengths.

| | Softball | 1 | 2 | 3 | 4 | 5 | 6 | 7 | 8 | 9 | 10 | TOTAL |
|---|---|---|---|---|---|---|---|---|---|---|---|---|
| **III. CONCERNING FUNCTIONAL CAPACITIES** (three to five best preferences) | | | | | | | | | | | | |
| **A. ORGANIZING TIME AND PERSONAL SPACE** | | | | | | | | | | | | |
| **19. Ordering My Time and Priorities** Consistently organizing my daily schedule to get the most important things done: appointments, deadlines, errands, projects, and the like. | ✔ | | | | | | | | | | | |
| **20. Ordering My Space** Keeping my surroundings well-organized and my household items in their place without much effort. Routinely putting things where they belong. | | | | | | | | | | | | |
| **B. BEING CREATIVE** | | | | | | | | | | | | |
| **21. Creating** Coming up with new ways to do things, improving routine tasks, looking at traditions with new viewpoints, questioning outdated regulations or procedures. | | | | | | | | | | | | |

| | Softball | 1 | 2 | 3 | 4 | 5 | 6 | 7 | 8 | 9 | 10 | TOTAL |
|---|---|---|---|---|---|---|---|---|---|---|---|---|
| **22. Imagining** Spending time imagining new stories, theories, and science fiction ideas, philosophical concepts, and the like (also referred to as daydreaming). | | | | | | | | | | | | |
| **23. Inventing** Originating new mechanical/technical gadgets, electronic devices, machines, chemical formulas, plant hybrids, and the like. | | | | | | | | | | | | |
| C. SUPERVISING OTHERS | | | | | | | | | | | | |
| **24. Initiating/Developing** Supervising others in starting new projects, programs, organizations, clubs, companies, and the like; also dramatically improving a program, company, etc. | | | | | | | | | | | | |
| **25. Long-Range Logistical Planning** Mapping out long-range details to meet my employer's, club's, family's, or church board's goals; finances, equipment, personnel schedules, etc. | | | | | | | | | | | | |
| **26. Managing** Supervising others in an "established" department, club, group, or organization over an extended period. | ✔ | | | | | | | | | | | |
| D. USING BODY, HANDS, FINGERS | | | | | | | | | | | | |
| **27. Being Physically Coordinated or Physically Active** Using my body, arms, and legs together, as in athletics, physical labor, construction work, and the like. | ✔ | | | | | | | | | | | |

| | Softball | 1 | 2 | 3 | 4 | 5 | 6 | 7 | 8 | 9 | 10 | TOTAL |
|---|---|---|---|---|---|---|---|---|---|---|---|---|
| **28. Using My Hands and Arms** Using my hands and arms and/or hand tools in activities, such as repairing or maintaining (car, furniture, clothes, equipment); building or assembling (cabinets, machines); using power tools. | | | | | | | | | | | | |
| **29. Operating/Driving** Operating or driving moving vehicles, such as a car, truck, farm/construction equipment, boat, aircraft, stationary equipment, machines, and the like. | | | | | | | | | | | | |
| **30. Using My Hands and Fingers** Using my hands and fingers for precision detail projects, such as building small scale model kits, soldering, jewelery casting, graphics paste-up, or drafting. | | | | | | | | | | | | |
| **E. HELPING OTHERS** | | | | | | | | | | | | |
| **31. Tutoring** Helping another person to cope with disabilities or learning problems, as in specialized training, coaching, tutoring, therapy, or rehabilitation over an extended period of time. | ✔ | | | | | | | | | | | |
| **32. Being of Service** Being most usually available to others when they need my help with their projects and programs to the neglect of my projects. | | | | | | | | | | | | |
| **33. Counseling** Patiently helping people over a period of time to resolve personal or emotional problems: dating, marriage, self-image conflicts; spiritual concerns; abnormal behavior. | | | | | | | | | | | | |

| | Softball | 1 | 2 | 3 | 4 | 5 | 6 | 7 | 8 | 9 | 10 | | TOTAL |
|---|---|---|---|---|---|---|---|---|---|---|---|---|---|
| **34. Reassuring and Supporting Others** Identifying with another's hurts and frustrations, giving encouragement, comfort, and support without necessarily trying to help them solve their problems. | | | | | | | | | | | | | |
| F. USING INTUITION | | | | | | | | | | | | | |
| **35. Evaluating People's Character** Accurately assessing others' integrity or sincerity, including motives, underlying thoughts, or attitudes, during initial encounters. | | | | | | | | | | | | | |
| **36. Making Future Projections** Accurately predicting the general public's response to future events, as in politics, clothing fads, business trends, or other future concerns. | | | | | | | | | | | | | |
| G. BEING PERSUASIVE | | | | | | | | | | | | | |
| **37. Negotiating** Successfully settling disputes between two or more people, acting as a go-between, arbitrating, negotiating contracts, being a peacemaker, or the like. | ✔ | | | | | | | | | | | | |
| **38. Selling** Successfully convincing others to buy and pay for a product or service, recruiting volunteers, fundraising. | | | | | | | | | | | | | |
| **39. Promoting** Successfully convincing others to accept a new idea or different viewpoint, changing people's minds about a particular product or service. | | | | | | | | | | | | | |

| | Softball | 1 | 2 | 3 | 4 | 5 | 6 | 7 | 8 | 9 | 10 | | TOTAL |
|---|---|---|---|---|---|---|---|---|---|---|---|---|---|
| **H. OBSERVING DETAILS** | | | | | | | | | | | | | |
| **40. Observing Physical Environment Details** Seeing details others often miss indoors or outdoors: street signs, rare plants, rock formations, animal tracks, and the like. | | | | | | | | | | | | | |
| **41. Observing Printed Details** Seeing details others often miss in written manuscripts, books, blueprints, and maps, including misspellings, "typos," or grammatical errors. | | | | | | | | | | | | | |
| **42. Observing in Three Dimensions** Visualizing a three-dimensional object from a two-dimensional drawing, such as a building from a blueprint, a cabinet from a sketch, a dress from a pattern. | | | | | | | | | | | | | |
| **I. USING NUMBERS** | | | | | | | | | | | | | |
| **43. Calculating** Quickly and accurately working with numbers and figures: adding, subtracting, multiplying, and dividing without much effort. | | | | | | | | | | | | | |
| **44. Recording and Auditing** Routinely counting and recording how many items are on a shelf, in a box, in a room, in a warehouse (taking inventory). | | | | | | | | | | | | | |
| **J. PROBLEM SOLVING PROCEDURES** | | | | | | | | | | | | | |

| | Softball | 1 | 2 | 3 | 4 | 5 | 6 | 7 | 8 | 9 | 10 | TOTAL |
|---|---|---|---|---|---|---|---|---|---|---|---|---|
| **45. Troubleshooting** Detecting mechanical, electrical, or technical problems, as in clocks, engines, electrical circuits, doorlocks—though not necessarily being skilled with tools. | | | | | | | | | | | | |
| **46. Solving Problems** Solving problems that come up at work, at home, in my hobbies, club meetings, activities, and the like (not necessarily mechanical or electrical problems). | | | | | | | | | | | | |
| **K. RESEARCHING FOR INFORMATION** | | | | | | | | | | | | |
| **47. Researching/Investigating** Collecting a lot of information from different sources about one or more subjects for present use or future reference (may include field research). | ✔ | | | | | | | | | | | |
| **48. Remembering** Recalling names, numbers, or other details quickly and accurately without much effort. | | | | | | | | | | | | |
| **49. Classifying** Routinely arranging and maintaining information, reports, photographs, or recipes for easy and quick reference (file systems, catalog systems). | | | | | | | | | | | | |
| **L. REASONING/CONTEMPLATING** | | | | | | | | | | | | |
| **50. Analyzing** Looking over an object to see how it is put together; studying a subject or opinion to determine its good and bad points and how it compares to other items. | ✔ | | | | | | | | | | | |

| | Softball | 1 | 2 | 3 | 4 | 5 | 6 | 7 | 8 | 9 | 10 | TOTAL |
|---|---|---|---|---|---|---|---|---|---|---|---|---|
| **51. Appraising/Evaluating** Accurately estimating the monetary value of a car, house, antique, collectable, or business opportunity and its economic potential. | | | | | | | | | | | | |
| **52. Synthesizing** Putting together different parts to make a whole, as in a project or report; selecting ideas, concepts, or objects in order to fit them together in a useful way. | | | | | | | | | | | | |
| M. MAKING DECISIONS | | | | | | | | | | | | |
| **53. Being Decisive** Spontaneously and skillfully responding to another person's accident or emergency situation, such as a child choking, kitchen fire, stalled car, or person drowning. | | | | | | | | | | | | |
| **54. Taking Risks** Committing my time or finances without undue stress, when there is an equal chance of success or failure. | | | | | | | | | | | | |

At this point I believe my three to five *functional* talent strengths are:

1. _____

2. _____

3. _____

4. _____

5. _____

## THE NEXT STEP

You have now completed all sections of the Talent Discovery Guide, and should have a good grasp of the way you communicate, the way you relate, and the way you function.

The next chapter will raise the question of leadership—an important subject but often misunderstood. Part of the natural abilities God gives to us is a capacity to influence others. We'll help you discover the way you lead and the opportunities God has given you to put your talents to good use for His glory.

## REFLECTIONS FOR YOUR JOURNEY

1. a. Summarize the teaching of John 13:34-35 and Hebrews 10:24-25 regarding helping interdependence.

   b. List two or three examples of how you might apply this teaching.

c. For believers who lack natural talent strengths in *helping* and *being of service* to others, how would you describe a basic adequacy (minimum) in this area?

2. People who have different strengths usually have different ways of doing things—whether they're mowing the lawn, furnishing a home, leading a meeting, or caring for a friend. What does Matthew 7:1-2 teach about the kind of attitude you ought to have toward people who are very different from you?

3. Select one of your *functional* strengths. Describe one way you could further develop this talent to a level of excellence (for example: take a course, read a book, interview others with this strength, go to a seminar, listen to tapes).

4. a. In which of your non-strengths do you think you should become more adequate? (Before making plans to improve in this area, review your conclusion with your group or a friend.)

b. Describe one way you could improve your adequacy in this area.

*For Group Discussion*
5. Choose one (or both) of the situations below and discuss your responses to these questions about the people involved: Who do you think is likely to be judgmental? Why? Who do you think is likely to feel guilty? Why? How might Romans 14:2-3 apply in this situation? (Discuss how you would advise the people involved.)

a. Barry excelled through school as an athlete and still plays tennis and basketball regularly. His fourteen-year-old son has no athletic ambitions; his twelve-year-old daughter demonstrates athletic aptitude far above average.

b. Charlene is engaged to be married in six months. Her mother, Pam, is concerned about Charlene's messy room and dirty bathroom. Pam is a "neat nick" house-keeper and an excellent cook. Pam would like to use her expertise to help Charlene prepare for her future role as a homemaker. Charlene shows no apparent interest in housekeeping or cooking.

# FIVE

# THE WAY YOU LEAD

L ook on the side of a hot water heater and you'll find a device called a *pressure relief valve*. If the water inside the tank gets too hot and begins to boil, this valve opens to release steam. If the valve fails to operate, the pressure will keep building until the water heater explodes.

Busy people need pressure relief valves, too. God has provided built-in physiological warning signs that indicate it's time to open a valve and let off steam. But often those signs are ignored.

When we allow too much pressure to build up inside us, we're heading for an "explosion." Some of us stop when we reach the peak of heat and pressure. Others of us go past that peak—to an emotional collapse, perhaps a nervous breakdown. Sometimes physical breakdown, such as a heart attack, stroke, ulcer, or high blood pressure, occurs.

Not a pretty picture, is it? If we knew it was coming, we'd certainly scramble to prevent it. Yet many of us willingly step into situations that set us on the path to such a crisis. We just don't see where we're heading. We end up wondering, Where did I go wrong?

## THE LEADERSHIP TRAP

One of the most common pressure-cookers in our world today is the pursuit of leadership positions. Our society as well as our Christian culture holds up leadership as a role we should all aspire to. Leaders are widely assumed to be the ones who do the "important" work.

The trap that many fall into is assuming that the only way to excel is to be a leader. And the only way to be a leader, the assumption goes, is to achieve success and recognition—to be accorded a certain position or status.

This kind of thinking is drummed into us from our earliest days. Report cards have blanks where teachers can indicate "qualities for leadership." Most youth measure success by such visible attainments as election to the student council, reaching the top rung of the popularity ladder, or becoming a team captain in a school sport.

Later on, we're urged to set our sights on "the top schools" or Ivy League colleges because they have the most status and "produce leaders." When we get out into the job world, we're under pressure to get promoted to higher and more responsible positions and titles as evidence of our achievement.

This pressure programs us to take advantage of *every* opportunity to become a leader. But when we don't get to be the class monitor in first grade, or win the leading role in the class play, or get elected to student government, or receive the promotion we were counting on, the message eventually comes through that we've failed. The conflict that results can push us into an identity confusion over our capabilities.

## PRESSURE RELIEF

How should we handle this pressure to attain leadership status? We have a few suggestions.

*Make sure you have a proper perspective of leadership.* This is one of the best ways to open a pressure relief valve, because there are so many misconceptions of leadership calling for our commitment.

One of the most common misconceptions involves our understanding of the way leaders function. This foiled reasoning assumes that *all leaders are supervisors*—that is, that leadership is defined by being "in charge." But this assumption shrinks leadership to a narrow and confining role.

People in leadership represent many roles and positions. We think these varied capacities are best understood in two categories that together define leadership rather than a narrow "in charge" definition.

1. *The leader as supervisor*—one who directs and oversees the activities and behavior of others. This is the traditional view of a leader.

2. *The leader as influencer*—one who influences the activities and behavior of others by demonstrating excellence. This can occur within any role, position, or title.

A leader can be a supervisor or an influencer or both, depending upon the individual. As you read through the following descriptions of these dimensions of leadership, look for areas that apply to you—even if you've never thought of yourself as a leader before. If you are now in a leadership capacity, use this material to get you thinking about how to make the most of your God-given strengths in this area of your life.

## THE LEADER AS SUPERVISOR

Let's look again at the natural abilities in the category of "supervising others," which you were introduced to in chapter 4. The three talents in this category best facilitate supervisory roles:

*Initiating/Developing (24)*—the capacity to coordinate the activities of others to start up new programs, systems, and projects. This is the talent for being a change agent. It is also called the entrepreneur talent and the "turn around" talent.

*Planning (25)*—the capacity to map out the long-range logistical details necessary to complete a project, giving consideration to time, costs, equipment, personnel, facilities, etc.

*Managing (26)*—the capacity to coordinate the ongoing activities of others in order to harmonize their efforts to accomplish a common goal. This talent is the main stabilizing factor in most organizations.

Initiators get things started. Then planners figure out the best way to get to where the team wants to go. Managers keep the whole process going in the most efficient way. All three are responsible for the coordination of the activities of others. Typical titles are president, director, manager, foreman, department head, and so on.

Surprisingly these talents appear to be mutually exclusive. We have not found anyone who excels in more than one of these areas. People who have a natural strength in supervisory leadership inevitably excel in one of these three areas and noticeably lack strength in another of these areas. For example, trailblazers (initiators) are usually not good maintainers (managers). Instead of establishing today's necessary policies and procedures, they are breaking ground—at least mentally—on some project for tomorrow.

But people who have a strength in any of these three areas still account for only 30 percent of the population, according to our studies. This does not mean that the other 70 percent do not have any leadership capacities. If you're part of this larger group, you will probably not be at your best as a leader who supervises others. However, you may choose to be a leader who *influences* others.

## THE LEADER AS INFLUENCER

The influencer exerts leadership by doing something well enough to set a standard or an example for others to follow or strive for. By excelling in the use of the talents you already have, you can attain a position of recognition on your job, in your church, or in your community. Once you are recognized for demonstrating excellence, others will come to you for your opinion, counsel, and advice. Doctors, lawyers, professors, and skilled craftsmen are examples of this type of leadership role.

But professional credentials are not necessary for this kind of influence. Consider Corrie ten Boom, subjected to the horrors of a Nazi concentration camp, who persevered in her faith and survived the ordeal. Her personal testimony, the books she wrote, and the movies made of her life extended her influence to millions of people.

You do not need an official position to be an influential leader. In fact, Jesus inverted the success/leadership position relationship when He said, "You know that the rulers of the Gentiles lord it over them, and their high officials exercise authority over them. Not so with you. Instead, whoever wants to become great among you must be your servant, and whoever wants to be first must be your slave" (Matthew 20:25-27).

We believe that serving others includes *using your God-given talents to complete tasks in as excellent a manner as possible*. "Whatever you do, work at it with all your heart, as working for the Lord, not for men" (Colossians 3:23).

*Each of us has natural talents that equip us to be an influential leader*. And the writers of Scripture repeatedly encourage us to a godly, influential leadership in others' lives.

To do your job the way God wants it done requires a commitment to excellence. Are you washing dishes? Clean them as though Christ were going to be the next person to eat from them. Are you a custodian? Set a standard of excellence in your tasks that will encourage others to strive for excellence in their responsibilities as well. Are you a parent? Strive for a godly influence in the lives of your spouse, your children, and those friends or acquaintances who enter your home.

## WHAT MAKES US SHRINK FROM LEADERSHIP

In the introduction to this book we summarized Jesus' parable of the talents, in which a master returned from a trip and rewarded his servants according to how well they had invested varying sums he had entrusted to them. Equal rewards went to the two servants who had excelled in carrying out their responsibility. "Well done, good and faithful servant," they were praised. But condemnation fell on the servant who shirked his responsibility out of fear and hid his sum in the ground. His master's indictment rings through to today: "You wicked, lazy servant."

Too many of us suffer from a cramped understanding of the nature of God. We picture Him condemning us if we step out and try. We fear failure and ridicule. This fear keeps us from investing the talents God has given us.

Some of us are too afraid we can never reach the "best," so we don't strive at all for excellence. This kind of perfectionism does no one any good. Remember: God doesn't want you to be *the* best; He wants you to be *your* best.

And then there is the self-defeating notion that we just don't *have* as much talent as others do, so the world really doesn't miss much if we never maximize what we've been given. The disobedient servant had been given only one talent (the others received two and five), so he probably thought, "It doesn't matter anyway." But it does. It's the difference between "Well done" and "You wicked, lazy servant."

If you have thought, "My contribution doesn't matter," you are in jeopardy of reacting in fear. Overcome your fears. Make a commitment to influence others by using your natural talents to their fullest.

## DISCOVERING THE WAY YOU LEAD

If you are not in a leadership position, consider your options. If you have *supervisory* talents, responsibility is probably lurking around the corner. If you will use and develop your natural talents, you can influence many.

If you do not have supervisory talents, remember that you don't need a position to be an influential leader. (On the other hand, don't try to escape all circumstances in which you will be asked to supervise others. If you're a parent, for example, you will be forced to achieve adequacy in this area.) Be careful not to define success as supervising others, and try not to let it become a major activity in your schedule. Keep at least 60 percent of your activities in areas of your natural strengths.

Keep in mind, if you will continue to follow Christ and grow more like Him, you can aspire to become a moral/spiritual leader ready for spiritual leadership responsibilities (either supervisory or influencing).

Whether it is in the church, community, government, or business world, trying to reach the top of the ladder can set you up for mounting pressure. God has His own ladder of success for you to climb. You are living successfully now if you are obediently striving to do your part the way God wants it done.

To get you thinking about improving in current leadership responsibilities or discovering new ones, take a few minutes to answer the following questions:

*Your Leadership Opportunities*
1. Based on past experience as well as your knowledge of your potential, check the appropriate box(es) describing your strengths in leading others:

*Supervisory*
❏ Initiating/Developing
❏ Planning

    ❏ Managing
    ❏ Influencing (State how you plan to influence.)

2. Briefly describe the kind of impact you want to have on others as you serve them in a leadership capacity:

3. List at least one to three leadership opportunities you see in your life, current or future, along with any thoughts you may have about how to make the most of them:

    a.

    b.

    c.

## THE NEXT STEP

In these first five chapters, you've unlocked and opened your sixth suitcase. You have step by step discovered its contents. You are now ready to learn how to take your suitcase on the road as you embark on your personal path to excellence.

In the second part of this book, we'll take you through key areas of life to help you apply your natural strengths to the day-to-day business of living. You'll be plotting the course of your own path—and we trust you'll be excited as you watch the road unfolding before you.

## REFLECTIONS FOR YOUR JOURNEY

1. Has this chapter challenged any of your previous concepts about your role in leadership? If so, describe your new thoughts or insights:

2. Read 1 Timothy 3:1-13. These are character performance standards, not talent expectations.

   a. *For those currently involved in church leadership:* In what areas do you need improvement?

   b. *For those not currently involved in church leadership:* What do you think might be the next step to prepare you for a leadership role within your congregation? (If you feel church leadership is not for you, explain briefly.)

3. Read Matthew 20:25-28. In what sense is a leader who supervises others a servant? (Hint: To supervise is to bring out the best in others.)

4. For each of the following environments, what advice would you give to those who have supervisory responsibilities but are not naturally gifted with *supervisory* talents?

a. At work:

b. At church:

c. At home:

*For Group Discussion*

5. Share with each other what you feel to be your focus on leadership: supervisory roles or influencing roles. Question, verify, and encourage each other as appropriate.

6. Once a person has achieved a level of recognized excellence in his or her field, brainstorm everyday opportunities for influential leadership, mentioning relevant Scripture passages as they occur to you.

PART TWO

# TAKING IT
# ON THE ROAD

# SIX

# YOU AND YOUR RELATIONSHIPS

iscovering the contents of their sixth suitcase can really get people excited. Some of them reconsider what their life is all about. If that kind of change is appealing to you, fine. If it's threatening to you, *relax*. There are plenty of opportunities to apply what you have learned without drastic changes in the lifestyle you already have in place.

In the remaining chapters, we'll be suggesting gradual changes that you can make in your life—involving personal relationships, your job, your church ministry opportunities, your recreational time. Of course, a series of little changes is one way to make a significant change—it just takes a little longer.

Perhaps the most important place to begin is with you and your most significant interpersonal relationships.

Significant relationships are usually a part of every other arena in life. In this chapter we'll ask you to single out one relationship. (You can repeat the process for others.) Then we'll help you explore how the contents of your sixth suitcase can affect the way you relate to this person.

The process of evaluating this relationship will include establishing actions or goals to improve it. This procedure may be too mechanical to use with everyone you know. However, completing it with one very special person will give you insights that you can take into other relationships. And the skill you acquire in using your knowledge of natural talents in relationships will help you in other areas as well.

## EXPLORING YOUR MOST SIGNIFICANT RELATIONSHIP

For this process of exploration, choose a person who is close to you in some way. If you're married, it is probably your spouse; if you're engaged, your soon-to-be spouse. You might select one of your children. If you are single, choose a close friend, a parent, a roommate, or an employer.

If there is more than one person you want to complete this exercise for, select one for the first time through. You can repeat the exercise later as many times as you wish.

This exercise is designed to help you understand how your relationship is influenced by the natural strengths and non-strengths of others. You'll be considering the other person's sixth suitcase, and comparing and contrasting it to the contents of your own.

Understanding each other's God-given talents is part of the foundation of a healthy relationship. It promotes better communication and encourages appreciation of the other as a unique individual. When two people harbor mistaken assumptions about each other's aptitudes, unfulfilled expectations are bound to cause conflict.

You may be choosing a relationship for this exercise

because you're aware of conflict in it and are hoping to gain insight. Be aware that your relational tensions may be due to sources such as personality differences or emotional baggage created by dysfunctional behavior. Knowing talent strengths will not heal the emotional and psychological effects of this kind of conflict, and this chapter is not designed for that level of help.

However, unacknowledged or unresolved talent differences *can* give rise to relational conflict. If this is the case in your significant relationship, then the exercise in this chapter may well help strengthen your relationship and facilitate healing of those tensions.

Our hope is that exploring the way talent strengths affect your relationship will ultimately provide a new sense of stability and depth. As you focus on how your strengths can complement each other, you may even begin to see a new way of looking at your relationship emerge from your reflections.

The following sections provide explanations of the four parts of the exercise: Evaluation, Affirmation, Dealing with Conflicts, and Appreciating Interdependence. Before reading farther, stop and familiarize yourself with the exercise itself, on pages 122-125 (but don't fill it out yet). Then come back and read these explanatory sections. Once you've read through them, you'll be well prepared to work through the exercise.

## EVALUATION

In this section you will be assessing the way your significant person communicates, relates, functions, and leads. You may want to review the Talent Discovery Guide sections you completed in chapters 2 through 4 and the section on leadership in chapter 5.

Try to stay with the same terms and talent definitions used in the earlier chapters. Be thoughtful, but trust your initial responses: you probably know this person quite well.

## AFFIRMATION

The second section of the exercise will encourage you to recognize and appreciate the talent strengths of your selected person.

Many of us unwittingly discourage our close friends from freely using their God-given talents. It can happen in a number of ways.

When a friend has strong abilities in the same area we do, it can make us feel insecure. Some people may respond to the threat by subtly condemning—or even overtly ridiculing—their friend's efforts. Their friend will soon stop using this strength in their presence, but will eventually resent this unnatural restriction. This causes tension to build.

An often subtle form of discouragement comes from a continual series of questions. "Why do you do it that way?" can imply, "You're doing it the wrong way." Those with *analyzing* or *problem-solving* talents usually ask in-depth questions for clarification. Unfortunately, many times these questions are misinterpreted as fault-finding. If you have a strength in *analyzing* or *solving problems*, be very careful in this area.

Discouragement can take many other forms as well: lack of confidence; withholding of necessary support, such as money for purchases or authority for making decisions; questioning qualifications; or simple failure to appreciate a job well done.

However, the means of encouragement are just as varied as the forms of discouragement. Consider these ideas for affirming a person close to you:

- Give praise for accomplishments.
- Let your person hear you tell others about his or her positive qualities or accomplishments.
- Buy gifts for this person that are compatible with his or her strengths.

- Express a desire to learn about the other person's interests in using his or her strengths.
- Look for ways to help this person develop those interests and strengths.

Be careful that your efforts are directed at *the other person's* encouragement. Seek your friend's good, not your own, by focusing on your friend's natural strengths, not on your own agenda for how your friend ought to behave or develop.

You might consider interviewing others who have talent strengths similar to those of your significant person. Ask them for specific suggestions on demonstrating affirmation and encouragement.

## DEALING WITH CONFLICTS

The closer relationships get, the more opportunity there is for competitive or combative attitudes. Sometimes this conflict arises from differences in natural abilities. This is what the third section of the exercise will help you explore.

In most marriages, the first few years gradually reveal that spouses see things from different perspectives. If the couple does not understand their talent differences, long-term conflict is likely to result—and therefore an unhealthy relationship.

The intimacy of marriage makes it fertile ground for conflict. But it is certainly not the only place where conflict flourishes. Any relationship can show wear and tear. Friendships that are pulled apart, church members who won't talk to each other, tension at the office—these may all reflect unresolved conflicts.

To help understand conflicts arising from talent differences, we'll look at a series of examples: husband and wife; pastor and elder; father and daughter; supervisor and employee.

*Bill and Sarah*
In chapter 1 we profiled Bill and Sarah, a married couple. We took you through the contents of their first five suitcases. Let's look at their sixth suitcase of natural talents.

Bill, who works as a design engineer, has *communication* strengths in *conversing* and *broadcasting* (via telephone); Sarah, who works as a homemaker and part-time florist, has strengths in *speaking in public* and *using colors and patterns*. On the surface these appear to be complimentary.

Since Bill does not have a strength in colors and patterns, he has little appreciation for money spent on interior decorating, landscaping, or stylish clothing. He frowns at spending extra dollars to keep up with current trends.

Sarah, on the other hand, is sensitive to the environment of a room, the exterior of her house, and the clothing she wears. For her, each of these areas sends a message to others. The wrong color would be like having a radio station turned on, full blast, but not tuned in correctly—constant static.

Like most young couples, when Bill and Sarah first discovered this discord they simply dismissed it as unimportant, because they felt their relationship was strong. But now, years later, Sarah lacks Bill's financial support in her area of strength. Her home environment is giving her headaches (others have testified to getting headaches from inappropriate decorating). She is upset at not having the freedom to purchase clothing as she did before she married Bill. (You guessed it, Bill still has a closet full of polyester leisure suits.)

Neither Bill nor Sarah understands that this conflict stems from the need they both have to operate according to their strengths. Bill's lack of support denies Sarah her need to express her *communication* strength. This denial will probably lead to resentment and further conflict unless the real issues are resolved.

Now let's look at Bill's and Sarah's relational strengths. Bill is *singular relational*; Sarah is *multi-relational*. Sarah has a large circle of many friends. Over time Bill can become critical of Sarah's "surface" treatment of people. He may develop an insecurity about her pattern of making friends more quickly than he does. Conversely, Sarah may criticize Bill for avoiding parties or not doing a better job as host when they have people over.

Bill and Sarah should be glad for their differences and capitalize on them by functioning as a team. Without a mutual appreciation of their strengths, however, they will probably become competitive and critical, rather than complimentary.

We have observed that *multi-relationals* and *singular relationals* tend to marry each other. These talents are complimentary. But without understanding and appreciation, the *multi-relational* usually tries to mold the *singular relational* into a "people person." The *singular relational* person tends to criticize the *multi-relational's* "shallow" relationships.

### Sam and Fred

Sam, the pastor, and Fred, the elder, are close friends. Fred is a business owner. He is strong in *supervising others*, specifically in being an *initiator*. Fred spearheaded the church growth and building programs, which Sam deeply appreciates.

Fred notices that Sam tends to be indecisive when dealing with staff performance problems. He thinks Sam spends too much time one-on-one with individuals in the church and not enough time providing a vision and direction for the congregation. He buys leadership books for Sam and pays his way to leadership conferences in an effort to help him in this area.

Sam appreciates Fred's comments. But he has also heard in confidence from some employees in Fred's company that Fred acts like a steamroller. They complain that Fred is not sensitive to people's needs and rarely takes time to listen to them. Some feel he is too focused on profits and forgets that people really make the company.

Sam's talents are in *being of service* and *reassuring and supporting*. He excels at encouraging people who are hurting. Fred is naturally able to see the big picture on projects and get people moving to accomplish goals *(initiating/developing)*. Their strengths complement each other beautifully.

Yet unless these two appreciate their differences and agree to a negotiated balance, over a period of time they can develop a combative standoff. If the church does not grow, Fred may blame it on a pastor who gets sidetracked by individuals and fails to set and pursue goals. Sam may point to Fred as an insensitive leader who drives people away.

### Sherry and Grant

Sherry, a high school freshman, and Grant, her dad, are planning Sherry's classes for next year. They're having trouble.

Sherry's drama teacher thinks Sherry has *acting* talent. She wants Sherry to use her electives to be in the school drama productions. Grant, a successful pharmaceutical salesman, thinks Sherry should be more practical. After all, life is not a stage play. Sherry will need the basics of a good education.

Sherry also has demonstrated strong athletic, *physical coordination*, ability. The track coach has encouraged her to think about working toward a possible college scholarship. But her dad is negative about this too. Sports are an "extra," he declares. First things first.

Sherry loves her dad but is finding it hard to trust his plans for her development. "But Dad, you just don't understand!" she pleads. "When I'm on stage or running track—well, I'm really alive! Don't force me to give them up."

Grant is strong in *conversing*, is *multi-relational*, and excels at *selling*. He also has strong numerical *calculating* and *remembering* strengths. He is unconsciously attributing his natural talents to his daughter (as most parents do), and so he assumes that she needs a certain curriculum and upbringing to make her way in the world. "After all, Sherry, I only want the very best for you," he explains. "When I was a kid we didn't have half the challenging career-oriented courses that are available to you today."

Father and daughter both have valid points, yet both need to bend. Grant needs to give Sherry opportunity to grow as God has gifted her. Sherry needs to recognize the validity of her father's concern that she build a practical foundation for college or future employment.

Without careful, sensitive assessment of his strengths and Sherry's, Grant could cripple their relationship. Sherry is not yet old enough to take the responsibility to negotiate and resolve conflict. Dad must take the lead to resolve the standoff for both of them.

### Margaret and Dave

Now let's shift to a boiling pot of misunderstanding: the workplace.

Margaret is a branch manager for State Savings and Loan. Dave has just been promoted to Margaret's branch as a commercial accounts manager.

Margaret, a *singular relational*, is strong in *writing, ordering time and priorities, analyzing,* and numerical *calculating*. She proceeds methodically before approving a loan and scrutinizes paperwork to ensure it's correct and complete. Dave, a *multi-relational*, is strong in *conversing, evaluating,* and *promoting*. He likes people and adopts a more informal approach to accepting loan applications. Both are accomplished professionals.

You can probably guess at some possible competitive and complimentary talent relationships. Margaret likes written and detailed reports. Dave prefers quick notes and conversation—the less paperwork, the better. Margaret is critical of Dave for his lack of thoroughness. Dave, frustrated with administrative procedures, is motivated to put deals together and make money.

How can Margaret and Dave make their strengths

work for rather than against each other in achieving company goals? Here's the advice we would give.

To Dave: Present your strengths to Margaret, how you work best, and why you have succeeded thus far in the company. Suggest how 60 percent of your time could be better used to meet the company's objectives.

To Margaret: Help Dave understand the importance of observing the policy for proper documentation. Consider giving Dave a part-time secretary who is good at writing reports. Recognize Dave's people strengths, and capitalize on them to bring in business for the bank.

Do you see that Margaret's and Dave's talents are very interdependent? What a team! And yet what a potential for a blow-up!

These examples only begin to illustrate the many possible combinations of talents that make up a relationship. If you and your most significant person don't acknowledge your talent strengths, it's just a matter of time before you start becoming critical or competitive. A strong mutual commitment to one another cannot endure the kind of daily friction in the above examples. Sooner or later separation will occur unless the conflict is openly discussed.

## APPRECIATING INTERDEPENDENCE

In the final section of the exercise, you will have opportunity to gain a new perspective on your relationship by focusing on your *interdependence.*

God has created each of us uniquely. No two people have the same fingerprints, or ear shape, or brain waves, or precisely the same combination of natural talents along with gender, height, hair color, and personality.

God has given each of us unique talent strengths. He has also chosen to create us with inherent limitations (nonstrengths) in certain areas. We can't do everything that needs to be done in a family, in a workplace, in a church ministry, in the community. God expects us to depend on the strengths of others as part of the resources we must draw on to carry out our responsibilities.

Each of us has something important to contribute in a significant relationship, and each of us has something important to receive in a significant relationship. That's the interdependent lifestyle God designed for us. And that's the way He expects us to live.

Unless you have healthy bonds with other people there is no way you can benefit from their strengths, nor they from yours. If you are insecure, manipulative, competitive, or defensive, not only will you miss the benefits of others' talents, but you will undermine your own confidence in the talents you have been given.

Imagine a lifetime of growing up with parents, or living with family members, or working for bosses, who tell you that you don't have a contribution to make. It's easy to see how a person in this situation can become insecure, defensive, and competitive. That is one reason these traits are indicators of a dysfunctional relationship.

One of the keys to breaking the bondage of a dysfunctional past is to begin to acknowledge that each person has God-ordained talent strengths. By acknowledging others' strengths, you can accept your own strengths and non-strengths. Those who have been the victims of the verbal abuse mentioned above need to be courageous enough to discover their natural talents and act on them. Then they can be appreciated and validated as the person God made. If you know people who have suffered this plight, you can make a major contribution by affirming and encouraging the development of their strengths.

In order to have a healthy relationship with your significant person, both of you need to appreciate your interdependence through a mutual sharing of strengths and compensation for non-strengths.

As you grow in your appreciation of the interdependent role you have with your significant person, you will also grow in your appreciation of the creative hand of God.

Your prayer life can be enhanced—there is so much to be thankful for when you thank Him for the differences! Intolerance hinders prayer because it keeps one from asking God's blessing on differences. Grow in appreciation of interdependence and you will grow in love for God.

## APPLYING YOUR SIXTH SUITCASE TO YOUR RELATIONSHIPS

You're now ready to work through the following exercise. Look for new perspectives on yourself as well as your significant person.

### EXERCISE: EXPLORING A SIGNIFICANT RELATIONSHIP

Person's Name _____

*Evaluation*
1. List what you believe to be this person's top two *communication* talent strengths. Refer to the chart at the end of chapter 2 for the list of talents.

   _____

   _____

2. List what you believe is the top *relational* strength of your most significant person (see chapter 3).

   _____

3. List the top three or four *functional* strengths of your most significant person (see chapter 4).

   _____

   _____

   _____

4. If this person ascribes to positions of leadership, are they influential, supervisory, or both? (See chapter 5.)

   _____

*Affirmation*

5. In the past, how have you reacted to this person's talent strengths? (Check any boxes that apply.)

   ❑ Encouraged their use.
   ❑ Remained neutral about them.
   ❑ Discouraged their use.
   ❑ Don't know.

6. Check the response that describes how often you currently encourage your most significant person to use his or her talent strengths. Then circle the goal you would like to set for yourself.

   ❑ Daily
   ❑ Every few days
   ❑ Weekly
   ❑ Monthly
   ❑ Hardly ever

7. Schedule a time to explain to your preferred person the talent strengths you have observed and your appreciation of them. Use specific examples from times you noticed this person using these strengths. Explain your strengths and how yours and his/hers work together. Make any notes now that come to mind about what you will say.

   If this level of interpersonal discussion is new to you, try a rehearsal before your discussion. Write out your thoughts word for word and record them on an audio cassette. Then play it back and listen to how you come across. *How* you say it will be just as important as *what* you say. Once you're relatively comfortable with your "script," ask your significant person to listen to you.

*Dealing with Conflict*

8. On the next page, record which of your preferred person's talent strengths are similar to yours. Next to each answer, jot down whether this similarity is currently functioning in a "competitive" or "complementary" manner.

_____

_____

_____

_____

9. a. Do your preferred person's strengths and desire to use them conflict with your strengths and your desire to use them? If so, briefly
describe these conflict areas.

b. What do you think is the best way to resolve these conflicts? Write
out your thoughts.

10. Set a time to discuss with your selected person the areas of conflict
or potential conflict that you have identified. Talk about your mutual
strengths and explain why using each of your strengths is important to
both of you. Be sure not to make accusations. Preface statements with "It
seems to me . . ." or "I feel that . . ."; avoid "You always . . ." "You do . . ."
claims. Jot down any thoughts about this that you have right now.

(Again, if this kind of conversation is awkward for you, practice by writing out your text, recording it on a cassette, and reviewing it before your
meeting.)

*Appreciate Your Interdependence*
11. Identify at least two ways *the strengths of your selected person* allows the two of you as a team to accomplish something you could not accomplish by yourself.

_____

_____

_____

_____

12. Identify at least two ways *your strengths* allow you and your significant person as a team to accomplish something your significant person could not accomplish alone.

_____

_____

_____

_____

13. Schedule a time with your selected person to talk about ways to encourage one another's strengths toward personal excellence.

Nice going. You have achieved a major relational milestone. Keep going.

## REFLECTIONS FOR YOUR JOURNEY

1. What is your best advice for someone whose significant person doesn't understand how God-given talents can contribute to a conflict?

2. Look back through your answers in the exercise evaluating your significant relationship.

   a. What potential obstacles do you see for discussing these issues with your significant person?

   b. What was the most helpful insight you gained in working through this exercise?

3. What advice would you give to parents for avoiding the trap of projecting their own talent strengths onto their children? (Hint: Start with promoting each child's strengths.)

4. Write down any specific ideas you have for . . .

   a. Expressing appreciation for your significant person's unique strengths:

b. Dealing with current conflict you may presently be experiencing:

c. Improving your attitudes or actions toward a richer and fuller interdependence in your relationship:

*For Group Discussion*

5. As group members, discuss the insights you have gained in your significant relationship. Include questions that came up, needs for further understanding, convictions regarding changes that need to be made.

    Respect each other's privacy and confidence. Many people have difficulty discussing their relationships, and no one should feel compelled to do so. Try to keep the direction of the discussion focused on how to apply sixth suitcase insights to significant relationships, with individual examples providing the framework for your interaction.

    If your group prefers to avoid a very personal discussion, choose one or more of the pairs provided as examples in this chapter—Bill and Sarah; Sam and Fred; Sherry and Grant; Margaret and Dave—and analyze their situation to come up with advice you would give them.

6. Brainstorm advantages of interdependence, citing examples wherever possible.

# SEVEN

# DOES ALL WORK MEAN NO PLAY?

ave you ever had the experience of running into old friends, perhaps at a class reunion, and feeling a twinge of envy at finding out how well they've done in their career?

Do you ever contrast yourself to someone you know who has just the kind of job you wish you could have? Or who has reached a level of professional accomplishment and satisfaction that makes you feel discouraged about where you are in life?

These feelings are rooted in the values our society powerfully reinforces. Values that proclaim that *whether* we work, and *how much* we earn or *how important* is our position, are directly tied to the worth of our contribution in life.

Next to your significant relationships, your work is probably the most important influence on your self-image, your relationship to God, and the way you perceive the contribution you make with your life.

## WORK AND WHAT YOU MAKE OF IT

Chances are good you will spend most of your life working, either inside or outside the home. With very few exceptions, most people do not have a choice in this matter.

How do you plan to invest the forty-plus hours you will be spending at work, every week, for the rest of your working life? You *do* have a choice here. You can assume victim status, and look at work as an unhappy necessity, or you can make your job a vehicle for expressing how God has gifted you.

Working only to meet expectations makes you a victim. Choosing work that allows you to grow as God has gifted you offers a totally different outlook. And homemakers, this chapter relates as much to your career as any others (later in this chapter we'll address homemaking specifically).

But what if the major part of your work does not draw on your talent strengths? Then you're spending a majority of your working hours contradicting the way God has gifted you. That's like constantly pruning a redwood tree that's designed to tower above the forest so that it really never has a chance to reach its potential. If the tree doesn't die, it will be forever stunted—which is far less than what God intended.

How should you evaluate your workplace in light of your natural attributes? Start by considering the following principles about the world of work.

## THE SIXTY-FORTY PRINCIPLE

The "sixty-forty principle" we have referred to in preceding chapters is a standard rule of thumb that John uses in counseling individuals who are making mid-career transitions. It goes like this:

*The best you can realistically expect for your work is*
*that 60 percent of your time will be spent on tasks that*
*draw on your natural talent strengths.*

This means that 40 percent of your time at work can consist of boredom, routine, red-tape, maintenance, clean-up, and hassle.

If you can develop the perspective that 60 percent is about as good as it's going to get, then you can relax without getting caught up in an unrealistic search for a big payoff. Yes, many are doing better than 60 percent, but only after they have settled into a compatible occupation and groomed it to fit them over a period of time.

Occasionally, there are frustrated individuals who come for counsel and complain about their jobs, but when it gets right down to looking at the assessment results, their current position is about as good as it's going to get. Their complaint is not with their employer; it's with the nature of life and work.

Accepting a job is like buying a house. In order to enjoy the benefits of home ownership, you also agree to put up with the responsibilities of owning that house. This includes home maintenance repairs, care for the yard, painting inside and out, replacing appliances, supplying furnishings, and all the rest. Then there is constant cleaning, scrubbing, and vacuuming. A person could become disillusioned about all these activities. It takes so much time to keep up a house. But most of us are happy to own our homes and take it all in stride. (Most, but not all.)

You should apply this same realism to your work. God has gifted you, but the world has not created a perfect slot for you. As you attempt to grow in your current job or seek a new one, the best you should expect is that you will apply the natural talents God has given you 60 percent of the time. Anything beyond that is a bonus. And remember—if you are not using your natural talents, no position or organization will meet your desire for career growth and development.

## IT AIN'T GONNA BE PERFECT

A second principle arises out of the Genesis curse (3:17-19). Because Adam sinned, God condemned him and mankind to earn his living by the sweat of his brow.

One of the consequences of the Genesis curse, then, is this simple principle: *It ain't gonna be perfect.* Work will not always be enjoyable. There will be exertion. There will be stress. There will be disappointments. This is one of the reasons for the sixty-forty principle.

Not only must we expect hardship, we must expect that diligent pursuit of our work can yield disappointment as easily as satisfaction. The one who succeeds does not always enjoy the fruit. It is God who rewards us with fulfillment and contentment (see this startling insight in Ecclesiastes 2:17-23, 5:18–6:2).

## THE GRASS ON THE OTHER SIDE OF THE FENCE

One of our favorite principles is, *The grass on the other side of the fence still needs to be mowed.* Those attractive opportunities out there still carry with them the basics of life—routine and maintenance. No career is completely free of the dregs of what life throws at us. We tend to jump at new opportunities looking only at upside potential, without considering downside risk.

It's like the two neighbors leaving for work at the same time. One reports to an office at 8:00 a.m., takes exactly one hour for lunch, and leaves at 5:00 p.m. The other owns a business, reports to no one but himself, and can (supposedly) work whatever hours he wants.

The first thinks to himself, "If only I had his job—what freedom! I'd be out of this grind." The second shakes his head, "Look at that guy! He goes to work in the morning and then leaves it at the end of the day; he doesn't have to bring it home, and it's not all up to him. I wish my life were that simple."

If these two were to switch jobs, chances are within a year the free life and the simple life wouldn't turn out the way they dreamed. They'd be longing for the grass on the old side of the fence.

## IS IT OUT THERE WAITING FOR YOU?

"It's out there waiting for you—go get it," the saying goes. We wish it were that easy.

When you go out searching for the ideal job, remember this principle:

> *The world is not waiting to give you a perfect slot for you to fill.*

Employers see tasks that need to be done; they are not looking for ways to make your life more fulfilling.

John and other IDAK counselors try to help clients realize that the job search process is not job *hunting* as much as job *negotiating*. With rare exceptions, employers create job openings defined by the needs of the organization, not by the needs and talents of potential employees. Clients are helped to negotiate to fill the employer's needs while still maximizing their unique strengths.

## HEY THERE, YOU WITH THE STARS IN YOUR EYES

Enthusiasm is a great thing. Getting carried away by enthusiasm is not.

When you're racing ahead with enthusiasm, stop long enough to remind yourself of this principle:

> *Passion or ambition can override common sense in selecting a career direction.*

It's natural to choose a job field because you like it very much, feel a "calling," and think the work is important. But these reasons are not enough. You must also factor in your natural talents. Consider the following diagram:

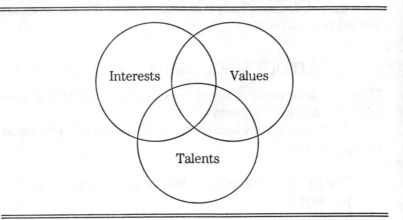

The ideal fit for your career direction is where the three circles intersect in the middle. Darken that triangle.

So be enthusiastic. Be passionate about your career goals. Don't compromise your ambition out of fear or fatalism. But *do* be realistic with your talents. Make sure you have not left your sixth suitcase behind in the trunk when you're getting out of the car to go to work.

## HOMEMAKING AS A CAREER

We now turn to a job field that needs its own consideration: homemaking.

Homemaking is a career choice and a valid occupation. It's been under attack in recent years, but it's also gaining back its lost respect. After all, this is a career that's been around about as long as any other, and it's never going to go away as long as men and women decide to raise children.

Let's get rid of the idea of homemaking as a duty and look at it from the perspective of a career allowing individuals to maximize their God-given capacities for excellence. This exploration of homemaking is important not only for wives but also for husbands.

*Homemaking and the Sixty-Forty Principle*
The following is a list some of the duties that the career of
homemaking can include. Any one of these could be developed into a major portion of a homemaker's daily routine.
Take a moment to check off the duties you as a homemaker
enjoy doing in your home (two or three of these could become
your 60 percent):

| | |
|---|---|
| ❑ Landscaping/Gardening | ❑ Purchasing |
| ❑ Interior Decorating | ❑ Educational Consulting |
| ❑ Doing Community Relations | ❑ Athletic Coaching |
| ❑ Repairing Equipment | ❑ Directing Youth Activities |
| ❑ Painting, Designing | ❑ Furniture Designing |
| ❑ Architectural Designing | ❑ Youth Counseling |
| ❑ Youth Employment Counseling | ❑ Needlepoint/Knitting |
| ❑ Gourmet Cooking | ❑ Writing |
| ❑ Caring For Pets | ❑ Bookkeeping |
| ❑ Reading | ❑ Antique Restoring |
| ❑ Researching | ❑ Photography/Video Production |
| ❑ Handcrafting | ❑ Picture Framing |
| ❑ Musical Performing | ❑ Vacation Planning |
| ❑ Historical Research/Recording | ❑ Home Hospitality |
| ❑ Bargain Hunting | ❑ Woodworking |
| ❑ Entertaining | ❑ Other_____ |
| ❑ Organizing Garage Sales | _____ |
| ❑ Remodeling | _____ |

Now let's go down a list of duties that are usually *not*
on the hit parade. Take a moment to check off the ones you
currently perform (these could make up your 40 percent):

| | |
|---|---|
| ❑ Changing, Laundering Diapers | ❑ Recycling/Disposing of Garbage |
| ❑ Washing Windows | ❑ Cleaning the Toilet Bowl |
| ❑ Disciplining Children | ❑ Laundry, Ironing |
| ❑ Cleaning the Oven | ❑ Paying Bills, Managing Finances |
| ❑ Putting Things Away, Filing | ❑ Cleaning up After Pets |
| ❑ Shuttling Kids to Activities | ❑ Weeding |
| ❑ Mending | ❑ Contending with Neighbors |
| ❑ Scrubbing Walls | ❑ Polishing the Silver |
| ❑ Making Beds | ❑ Repairing the Gutter |
| ❑ Painting the House | ❑ Other_____ |
| ❑ Vacuuming, Dusting | _____ |
| ❑ Washing Dishes | _____ |

Think about these two lists. We've attempted to separate the 40 percent that is usually perceived as the dull, boring, routine maintenance of homemaking away from the possible 60 percent in which you as a homemaker have an opportunity to express your natural talents and grow as a person.

Your natural talents can be matched to certain home duties to provide a sense of purpose and personal growth. As a matter of fact, you can weave most of the nurturing and discipling of your children around your specialty—whether it is gardening, knitting, music, pets, or anything else.

*Developing Your Career of Homemaking*
To develop your homemaking career, select the homemaking duties that you consider enjoyable and that are matched to the talents you discovered in the first part of this book. These activities can become your unique focus as a homemaker, your channel to develop who you are as a person and how you will express that identity in service to God and others.

Developing your natural attributes will require the support of your spouse—in most households, this means the working husband. This support requires the spouse's *participation*—for example, in freeing up funds to buy equipment, freeing up time by helping out with household chores or by caring for young children. Supporting a wife's strengths means aiding her in the pursuit of her 60 percent and filling in as necessary with doing chores in her 40 percent.

This is part of the interdependence discussed earlier. The homemaker supports her husband in his work, and the husband needs to support her in her work. And as soon as the children are old enough, they should pitch in as well. As you establish a pattern of interdependence, your children will begin to observe your enthusiasm for developing yourself and your aptitudes. They will recognize that they have natural aptitudes as well. You won't have to convince them that God has gifted them; they will already see it modeled in you.

The converse is true as well. If you are a harried homemaker, constantly running around cleaning up after everyone and hating it, your children will notice it and make assumptions accordingly. Your sons may develop the idea that women are supposed to pick up after them. Your daughters may feel trapped. In some supposedly spiritual circles the men still expect to sit down to eat a home-cooked meal at their convenience, just the way Mom used to do it, even if their wife is holding down a full-time job.

Some of you homemakers may be feeling somewhat discouraged right now, because your experienced guess is that your husband or children will probably not cooperate. There is still hope! You can choose to use your discretionary time to focus on one of your preferred activities. Look for opportunities, however small, during your daily or weekly routines to slip in some activity related to your talents. Once it begins to blossom you can attempt to recruit support to get more time and resources to continue your growth.

## TAKING YOUR SIXTH SUITCASE TO WORK

You are now ready to evaluate your current job. If you find a high level of compatibility, you probably should continue in your present position. However, lower levels of compatibility will most likely require an outlet for talent expression and growth through extracurricular activities in your church, through hobbies, community service, and/or activities with ministry organizations. For extremely low levels of compatibility, a new job or new career may be indicated.

The hours you spend at work are a significant part of your life. Hating to get up in the morning because it means starting your job will eventually have a very profound impact on your emotional and physical health. Therefore, you need to evaluate carefully whether your work is allowing you to grow as an individual, or whether your work runs contrary to the way God has gifted you.

The following exercise will help you evaluate your current job, whether you're working inside or outside the home.

---

### EXERCISE: EVALUATING YOUR WORK

1. List the five primary duties included in your present job (where you spend most of your time).

   a. _____

   b. _____

   c. _____

   d. _____

   e. _____

2. Evaluate these five job responsibilities to decide what kinds of talent strengths they require (so you can compare them to *your* natural talents in question 3 of this exercise).

   As you decide what *communication, relational, functional,* and *supervisory* strengths are necessary for excelling in the job responsibilities in your work, please refer back to the charts in chapters 2 through 4. Use the talent names and definitions from those sections of the Talent Discovery Guide to answer this question.

   a. List the *communication* talents that are absolutely essential for the performance of your work duties (see list on pages 61-63).

      (1) _____

      (2) _____

      (3) _____

   b. List the single most critical *relational* talent that your work requires (see list on page 69 or 74). Occasionally job duties will require equal performance in all three *relational* areas. This will cause a considerable amount of stress. Each job should have one dominant mode of relating to people if a person is to excel.

   _____

c. List no more than three essential *functional* talents that are required for peak performance in the work duties you have listed above (see list on pages 81-87 or 89-95).

(1) _____

(2) _____

(3) _____

d. Are *supervisory* strengths required for these job responsibilities?

❏ No
❏ Yes—which one? _____

3. Next you will evaluate how your natural talent strengths compare with the required talents you just listed in question 2. (Note: A realistic view of employment positions is that a match in two of your "top" talent areas is a very good match.)

   Now compare the talent strengths you listed in question 2, above, with the talent strengths you discovered in yourself in chapters 2 through 5.

   Do you have any matches? If so, list them here:

_____

_____

If you did discover any matches, consider yourself blessed. Be confident in your position and continue to grow in it.

   If you did not find any matches, or are not sure, answer these questions:

a. Write down any thoughts you have about how you might negotiate some of your duties so that they will better fit the talents you have.

b. Should you consider looking for a new position?

❏ Yes
❏ No
❏ Not sure—need advice or further exploration
❏ Too early to tell

Now that you've evaluated your current work responsibilities against the contents of your sixth suitcase, we'd like to give you some tips on maximizing the compatibility between your job and your talents.

## NEGOTIATING TO USE YOUR NATURAL TALENTS

Because your work is so critical in confirming the identity God has given you, and has such a high potential for fostering or undermining your personal growth and development, we want you think about how to improve your work compatibility through *negotiating*.

Unfortunately, the term *negotiating* is sometimes used in a negative way, connoting manipulation or trying to get the best of someone else. We're using the term in the positive sense of reaching for alternatives that may be in both your best interests *and* those of your employer or spouse.

Before you begin the negotiating process you must look at things from your employer's (or spouse's) point of view. What do they stand to gain and what do they stand to lose from the changes you're suggesting? You should clearly document the advantages to the changes you suggest—and make sure they outweigh the disadvantages.

One of the best preparations is to role play your recommendations and strategy with a trusted friend before talking with your employer or your spouse. This will give you a chance to revise your comments and suggestions while receiving feedback. If you have major points to negotiate, it's better to plan only one point per session, rather than dumping the truck all at once. Check the suggestions and negotiating principles in chapter 10 of this book before you begin the actual negotiating session.

## HANDLING THE MARGINAL AREAS

"Marginal Areas" are those parts of your job that you see as not great but also as not all that bad. We want to help you learn how to better live with them.

An example of a marginal area could be your role in a family-owned business: your job is critical and fixed, so you don't really have the option of negotiating or leaving it. Another example is if you're in a tenured position and have just a few more years to retirement. You may not want to leave now and lose a valuable financial asset.

Of course, if a marginal area gets bad enough you may well have to consider leaving it—but then it becomes an issue of job change, which we'll look at soon. But right now we're assuming situations in which the balance tips in favor of staying with it.

One way to live with marginal areas is to do an end run. If the satisfaction in the job is so-so, then look for maximizing your strengths outside the job. Develop your talents during your discretionary time.

With careful management of your discretionary time, you can attain an overall goal of spending 60 percent of your week in the areas of your natural ability. You just can't expect that all or almost all of that 60 percent will occur at work.

For example, ministry through a local church can provide almost endless opportunities for exercise of strengths in areas of personal interest and high value to you. This area alone can make up the deficit of talent use that you must live with on the job.

Other opportunities for talent development off the job include hobbies, extracurricular activities, volunteer time with ministry or community organizations, sports, or continuing education programs. When your work does not allow you to express your strengths, these alternative expressions can be important channels for getting you to a sixty-forty position.

However, these activities are important in their own right, whether or not you are hitting the sixty-forty level on your job. And they should not be used to prop up a sagging job situation that needs to be changed. Your work should *not* be a stress-filled drain, denying your strengths and highlighting your non-strengths.

In the next two chapters we'll spend a lot more time on these areas of ministry and discretionary time. For now, let's keep them in mind as a resource for compensating a less-than-ideal work situation.

## WHEN IT'S TIME FOR A CHANGE

And then there comes the moment when you know it's time for a change. Negotiation is inadequate to address the imbalances; accepting the position as "marginal" is unhealthy for you in the long run. You've ridden it as far as you can, and now you need a new horse.

Whether you need a *job* change or a *career* change depends on the particulars of your situation. If your natural talents don't match those required in your current field, you may need to change careers. However, if your talents do fit in the career you're now in, but your employer does not allow you to express them appropriately, you probably need a new employer.

From our experience in counseling people through job changes, here are the crucial guidelines to follow when contemplating such a move:

1. *Write down the advantages and disadvantages of your current job.* Write down whatever you are thinking. It will force you to clarify your thoughts and enable you to arrange them in a logical order.

Reviewing what you've written, either by yourself or with another person, will often give you enough distance to understand and critique your reasoning. You'll be more quick to detect "potholes" in your judgment, and you'll be better able to confirm where your thinking is on solid ground.

2. *Get input from others.* Are you being realistic? Find those who can help you clarify your thinking, offer ideas, or give you additional information. Those in your career field

can confirm or challenge your evaluation of talents needed to do your job. Friends or close acquaintances who know you well can be very helpful at this stage.

Make sure that you do not depend on others' feedback to provide a decision for you, however. *You* should be the one to determine what you will do next.

3. *Reach agreement with your spouse.* Ideally, married people function as a team. Decisions of this gravity should reflect that teamwork.

Agreement from your spouse should be more than simple acquiescence—"Yeah, fine, I'll go along with you." There should be genuine enthusiasm for the decision between you. Otherwise, you may find a lack of support at a crucial juncture.

If your spouse does not agree with you, wait and continue to dialogue. God's timing may be a little later than you want. If you remain convinced you need to make a change but your spouse still objects, proceed with great caution. Get plenty of godly counsel before doing anything.

In summary, use this checklist to confirm your decision that you must make a change. If you can check all the items on the list as present in your current situation, then you can proceed with a fair degree of confidence in pursuing new employment.

*Job Change Checklist*
❑ Employer's demands do not allow you to reach the 60 percent level.
❑ Repeated efforts to negotiate change have failed.
❑ Confirmation of your evaluation by at least three people.
❑ If married, agreement from spouse.
❑ You have discovered something better that is confirmed by spouse and others.

Seeking professional counsel should not be the first place you turn, but it certainly should not be a last resort. Consider investigating these resources if you feel the need.

There are many more mid-career-change counselors with experience today than ten years ago. For a list of trained and certified mid-career-transition counselors in major cities throughout the United States and Canada, write to:

The IDAK Group
Banfield Plaza Building
7931 NE Halsey, Suite 309
Portland, OR 97213-6755
(503)252-3495

## WHAT YOU HAVE TO DO, WHAT YOU WANT TO DO

The expression "all work and no play" implies that work is drudgery—the stuff you *have* to do. Play, on the other hand, is the activity you *want* to do—what you enjoy.

Our hope for you is that *your* job will become the place in which you work hard *and* play hard. May it be an area of your life in which you rise to challenges, achieve the discipline of effective routine, and find freedom in the things you enjoy and naturally do well.

So go for it, and take your sixth suitcase with you.

## REFLECTIONS FOR YOUR JOURNEY

1. When you are experiencing stress, how can you tell whether it's due to the ordinary demands of life (which we are equipped to handle) or to work responsibilities that are not matched to your talent strengths (which can burn us out)? Write down your thoughts.

2. Imagine what your work situation would look like if you consistently achieved the sixty-forty level of compatibility with your talent strengths. Write out a brief description of this picture—whether actual or hypothetical.

3. Do you feel the need to make any changes in your work situation in order to improve compatibility with your talent strengths? If so, write down your thoughts concerning each of the following.

   a. Adjustments you can make on your own:

   b. Changes within your current situation that you will need to negotiate with your boss:

   c. Changing jobs or career fields:

*For Group Discussion*
Share with each other your insights regarding job compatibility, or use the following list of questions to stimulate discussion and interaction. Decide as a group which of the following questions you want to focus on, or break up into smaller groups according to interest and choose the appropriate category of questions.

*Questions on negotiating job responsibilities:*
4. a. What are your biggest obstacles to negotiating your desired changes?


   b. What do you think are the best ways to overcome them?


5. Role play a sample negotiating strategy (ask someone in the group to offer his or her situation for this exercise) and critique the encounter.

*Questions on homemaking:*
6. What homemaking tasks provide you with the greatest sense of personal growth and enrichment?


7. a. How would you suggest a wife plan for a change in her role as a homemaker to reach the 60 percent level?

b. What steps do you suggest for the husband?

8. What are the key factors a couple should consider in deciding whether both spouses will work outside the home?

9. What training courses or seminars are available in your local church or community to enrich the role of the homemaker?

*Questions on changing jobs or career fields:*
10. Discuss in general terms what kinds of conditions would indicate a "yes" or "no" decision when considering a change in jobs or career fields. (Review the job change checklist on page 143. Is there anything you would add to this list?)

11. Share with each other your plans or questions regarding job change. Help each other clarify issues, identify pros and cons, and brainstorm strategies and opportunities.

# EIGHT

# MINISTRY:
# DO IT THE EASY WAY

here's a place in your community that's just waiting for you to put your talents to use. It will offer endless opportunities for personal and spiritual growth in service to others. You can flourish there as an individual, united with others in common pursuits. You may even make some lifelong friends. And there will always be a place just for you, an opening no one else can fill. All you have to do is walk in and let them know you're here.

It's called *your local church.*

We strongly believe that the Bible encourages believers to draw together in communities of commitment, to blend their strengths in a way that honors the Lord. This kind of union offers strength and protection amid spiritual warfare; encouragement and challenge in shared joys and struggles;

guidance and support in reaching out to others. It happens when a group of people know they need each other and promise to stick together.

Involvement in your local church is a unique opportunity to use your natural talents in a way that complements and builds on the strengths of others. It will draw you out of yourself in a healthy sense. Without this involvement, you may drift out of the life of a church into a passive posture. Few people will really get to know you, and as relationships remain shallow you may tend to drift from one congregation to another, wondering why you just don't seem to "fit in."

We're here to tell you that you can always find a place to "fit in" at your local church.

Of course, you may be smarting right now from someone's attempt to *make* you fit in. If you've suffered volunteer abuse, you may be thinking, "Never again!" This can happen when people who volunteer are overworked and underappreciated, or are pressured into tasks they're not suited to and don't enjoy.

One of the most effective ways to resist pressure to accept positions for which you are not wired is to aggressively pursue roles that are suited to you. Your new understanding of your natural talents should help you find your niche—or help you create a new niche.

In a church setting, just as in your work, you should pursue a role that draws upon your interests, values, and talents. But here you will be under the authority of current leadership. Implementing your chosen outreach is not always an easy goal to accomplish, especially if the contribution you want to make is something that's never been done before. This chapter will help you find ways to communicate your ideas effectively to church leadership.

Group support is an important asset for persisting and developing credibility. Others in the group will help you clarify your thinking. They will validate your conclusions. They will give you a forum to practice verbalizing your plan.

They will keep you keeping on. They will anticipate obstacles, and perhaps help remove them. And most importantly, they will pray for you.

If you are working through this book alone rather than with a small group, find a friend from your church who will meet with you on a regular basis for the next few weeks as you complete the exercises in this chapter. Even if your friend is not familiar with this book, his or her support could be invaluable. (If you want help in getting your church involved, the IDAK Group has developed this material into a popular church seminar. See address on page 144.)

The following section will lead you through an exercise in developing a plan for ministry through your local church. Once you have a vision for how to match your talents to the needs of your congregation, we'll help you prepare for proposing and implementing it.

## EXERCISE: FIVE STEPS
## TO YOUR OWN MINISTRY PLAN

*Step One—Choose an Activity*
Select three ministry activities (see following lists) that utilize your *communication* and *functional* strengths. Your *relational* strengths will not necessarily be a factor in choosing one activity over another at this time.

This list of ministry options is a drop in the bucket compared to all the possibilities. We've included it to prime your creative pump. Feel free to add other activities as they occur to you.

| PERFORMANCE ACTIVITIES | PUBLIC RELATIONS/ PROMOTIONAL ACTIVITIES |
|---|---|
| ❑ Drama | |
| ❑ Humor Narratives | ❑ Advertising |
| ❑ Music | ❑ Bulletin Board |
| ❑ Public Reading | ❑ Church Newsletter |
| ❑ Puppetry | ❑ Greeting |
| ❑ Storytelling | ❑ Promoting |
| ❑ Other _____ | ❑ Ushering |

❑ Visitation
❑ Other _____

SERVICE ACTIVITIES
❑ Building and Grounds Operation
❑ Bookkeeping
❑ Carpentry, Electrical, Mechanical
❑ Gardening, Landscaping
❑ Transportation (Driving Youth, Handicapped, Shut-ins)
❑ Painting
❑ Library Operation
❑ Nursery Care
❑ Office Administration
❑ Food Preparation
❑ Recording/Duplicating Tapes
❑ Vehicle Maintenance/Repair
❑ Lighting, Sound System
❑ Other _____

TEACHING ACTIVITIES
❑ Outdoor Recreation, Retreats, Camps
❑ Home Study Groups
❑ Adult Sunday School
❑ Youth Sunday School
❑ Children's Sunday School
❑ Continuing Education Courses
❑ New Member Classes

❑ Long-Term Courses
❑ Short-Term Courses
❑ Other _____

SUPPORT ACTIVITIES
❑ Caring for Needy
❑ Counseling
❑ Nursing Home Chaplain
❑ Hospital Chaplain
❑ Telephoning
❑ Prayer Chains
❑ Tutoring
❑ Visitation
❑ Missions Correspondence
❑ Other _____

SPECIALTY ACTIVITIES
❑ Bulletin Preparation
❑ Handicrafts
❑ Exterior Decorating
❑ Interior Decorating
❑ Graphic Design
❑ Flower Arranging
❑ Photography
❑ Researching
❑ Chronicling, Recording History
❑ Computer Systems Support
❑ Other _____

*Step Two—Narrow the Field*
You should now have three activities to consider. The second step is to define them more specifically, narrowing them to concrete ideas rather than general areas of interest. The way to do this is by sharpening the focus of the activity to reflect more of your *functional* talents.

For example, if you selected bulletin preparation as an activity, and one of your *functional* strengths is *creating*, you may want to step into a position allowing you to innovate some new formats. If you chose church newsletter as an activity and you are strong in *initiating/developing* and supervisory leadership, you could plan the launch of a newsletter and recruit others for a newsletter staff committee, which you would chair.

Ready? Write out your final refinements to your selected activities.

*My preferred church ministry activities are:*

1. _____

2. _____

3. _____

*Step Three—Choose an Audience*

"Audience" refers not to those who will watch you in action, but to those who will benefit from your actions.

If your activity does not immediately involve a particular person or group of people (e.g., bookkeeping, running the sound system), skip this step and go on to step four.

If your planned activity does include people as part of its immediate focus, select those toward whom you would like to direct your ministry. Your people focus may or may not reflect your *relational* talents. A ministry directed toward college students, for example, can be in a *singular relational, multi-relational,* or *familiar group relational* role.

---

MY PREFERRED AUDIENCE IS
(one primary focus):
- ❑ Adults (indicate age level)
- ❑ Senior citizens
- ❑ Career singles
- ❑ College students
- ❑ Teens
- ❑ Children (indicate age level)
- ❑ Infants
- ❑ Newly married
- ❑ New members
- ❑ Business and professional men
- ❑ Business and professional women
- ❑ Families
- ❑ Mothers of young children
- ❑ Single parents
- ❑ Community neighbors
- ❑ Missionaries
- ❑ International students
- ❑ Ethnic groups, refugees
- ❑ Unemployed
- ❑ Disabled, handicapped
- ❑ Abuse victims
- ❑ Homeless
- ❑ Shut-ins
- ❑ Addicts
- ❑ Victims of dysfunctional families (codependents)
- ❑ Other _____

---

*Step Four—Choose a Setting*
What kind of environment do you envision as the setting for your ministry activity? Where should your activity take place in order to maximize the effectiveness of your efforts and integrate well with your schedule?

Choose three locations from the list below as your first, second, and third choices for the setting of your ministry (indicate by writing in a "1," "2," or "3" next to the boxes).

Your selection of activities and audience will have a bearing on the setting but will not necessarily dictate it. A ministry to college students, for example, could be done on campus, in a student center, in a home, or at the church building.

| MY PREFERRED SETTINGS ARE: | ❑ School campus |
| --- | --- |
| ❑ Church building—Sunday morning | ❑ Hospital(s) |
| ❑ Church building—Sunday evening | ❑ Playground/park/recreation center |
| ❑ Church building—weekday | ❑ Prison |
| morning/afternoon/evening | ❑ Retirement home or full-care home |
| ❑ Community (specify location) | ❑ Your home or another's home |
| _____ | ❑ Other _____ |

*Step Five—State Your Purpose*
Combine your responses from steps one through four into a statement of purpose by filling in the blanks below.

*I would like my church ministry thrust to be directed to _____ (people focus) by doing the following: _____ (specify one ministry activity) at _____ (setting).*

## GETTING IT OFF THE GROUND

You have a plan—congratulations! The final statement you concluded with in the above exercise should reflect you as God made you: a unique individual, uniquely prepared to carry out His purposes in the world. Now it's time to take the next step in getting it off the ground. Welcome to the process of converting ministry *purpose* into ministry *reality*.

Good planning begins with *optimism*. If you let yourself slide into the "it will never work" mentality, your subconscious will take over to assure that your "never work" conclusion is correct. Think positively!

To help you get your ministry off the ground mentally, try a little exercise in creative visualization. Bracket out all the known realities and imagine that everyone at your church is waiting with bated breath to hear what you have to say. You don't have to dance around any hot spots, couch your terms, or work around obstacles. There *are* no obstacles. Your church is eager to welcome you, support you, encourage you. They recognize that God has gifted you, and that there is a desperate need for your contribution, just the way you are.

Such enthusiasm will spur you on to develop a plan worthy of their response. Now you are ready to develop your proposal.

## TEAMING UP WITH A PARTNER

It is difficult to create plans that are complete and credible when you're working all by yourself. We suggest you find a friend who is willing to do the same ministry at the same time and location to the same people.

A primary goal of your teamwork with this ministry partner is mutual encouragement. Choose a friend or acquaintance you enjoy being with—someone from a study group or from your congregation. This person should have a passion to reach out to the same people you do. From now on, meet with your partner to discuss the development of your plan for ministry.

Make your plan as complete as possible. Start with the statement you wrote in the above exercise, and expand from there. Include as many details as possible to help you think ahead and anticipate adjustments. Don't be afraid to think big, but don't bite off more than you can chew in this initial phase. If you envision a fully-staffed crisis counseling clinic in the future, for example, your plan may begin with you and your ministry partner making your *counseling* strengths available for a two-hour session on Tuesday evenings.

## PREPARING A PROPOSAL

Use your ministry partner and your small group (if you're part of one) to help you incubate your plan. This kind of reinforcement is important. Your plan, as with anything new, requires a certain amount of time to secure itself and withstand criticism. In virtually all successful enterprises and ministries the originator establishes principles, develops prototypes, and experiments with concepts or products before presenting anything to the public.

As an introduction to your proposal, restate your natural talents and your ministry purpose (see sample proposal, next page). Then in the major part of it, state clearly and specifically what you want to do and how you plan to carry it out. If your plan includes a new activity, call it a pilot project that would be done for a short term and then evaluated for its effectiveness.

Support your proposal with reasons why you want to initiate this particular activity. Include both your qualifications and the benefit it will be to the church. Help people buy into your idea by explaining why you are so excited. Your proposal will receive more careful consideration when others sense your passion for it.

When you describe proposed activities, be as thorough as possible. If you want to teach a Sunday school class, which one? If you plan to drive the church bus, when? Where? If your plan is a further development of a current routine, make a small adjustment suggestion, not an overhaul: "I propose driving the bus and leaving ten minutes earlier to allow for an extra stop at Hillcrest Nursing Home where there are two people I know who would attend our worship service." This kind of thoroughness will show that your plan is workable.

Include where and when this ministry is going to take place. "I plan to carry out this ministry in my home, on Tuesday evenings." Or, "I plan to do this at the church building on Sunday nights." Or, "I plan to do this while accompanying the high school youth retreat." Explain why you chose this preferred place and time.

Establishing your proposed plan may take more than one week. Usually you will have parts of it clear while other aspects need more details or supportive reasons. Your ministry partner should help you by adding suggestions and amplifying your thoughts.

The following sample proposal provides an example to help you visualize what form your own proposal will take.

---

## A SAMPLE PROPOSAL

### MY PLAN
By Pete Brown

MY NATURAL TALENTS
My communication strengths are: *moderating, teaching*
My relational strength is: *familiar group*
My functional strengths are: *creativity, problem solving, tutoring, and being of service*

MY MINISTRY PURPOSE
I would like to *disciple new converts* by leading small group Bible study and discussion at *my home or a friend's home on Tuesday evenings from 7:00 to 10:00.*

MY PROPOSAL
*I propose a pilot project of one six-week study for new converts and new members using* Lessons on Assurance *study material. This material teaches young believers five foundations of the Christian life. It is appropriate for new members because in a short period of time they can be evaluated and then directed toward programs in the church that meet their needs. Too often in times past we assumed new members already had these foundations and later discovered they did not.*

*During each session there will be opportunities for discussion. I plan to add games or exercises that help people understand the Bible passages being studied.*

*The meeting is to be held at David and Cynthia Blare's home. They are a gifted host and hostess and have agreed to this plan. Their home will provide a relaxed atmosphere conducive to closer personal relationships. I propose that the group meet there on Tuesday evenings from 7:00 to 10:00 with light refreshments.*

*It will be my responsibility to recruit church members for this meeting. I will use the time before and after the worship service to make contact with prospects and follow up on them with phone calls and personal visits as necessary. I anticipate recruiting six to ten people for this pilot.*

*The project should be evaluated by my church's pastoral staff. If this pilot is judged successful, this study group will be repeated on a regular basis; I suggest four times during the first year.*

## PRESENTING YOUR PROPOSAL

After you've prepared your proposal, put it through a dry run by presenting it to your ministry partner or study group. Feedback from the dry run can help point out where additional information might be helpful, identify potential obstacles and how to overcome them, or anticipate responses from church leadership.

As you prepare for your dry run and final presentation, use your *communication* strength. If you're strong in *writing words,* write it out, word for word, then type it up and make copies for your reviewer(s) and church leaders. If you are talented in *speaking, teaching,* or *giving presentations,* then prepare to stand up and explain your plan for ministry. Consider using visual aids, such as a flip chart, marker board, or blackboard, especially if you have *artistic* strength. Illustrate the concepts using circles and boxes and triangles and so forth. If you have *broadcasting* talents you may want to record your presentation on audio cassette for your practice session.

Continue to polish your proposal until you believe it really communicates clearly what you want others to understand. Acceptance of your plan will be directly related to how clearly and convincingly you communicate your ministry idea.

It makes sense to bring your ministry partner to make your final presentation with you. Your proposal should take about five minutes to explain to church leaders. Plan for at least ten minutes after that to allow questions and discussion.

## DO IT YOUR WAY

You can't rush through the planning steps suggested in this chapter and come up with a thorough proposal. But with prayer, preparation, teamwork, and enthusiastic effort, you *can* step out into the arena of ministry. You'll have the confidence that you are moving ahead into an area for which God has qualified you.

May you find yourself on the path to excellence as a vital and contributing member of your local church. Once you've tasted the freedom and satisfaction of doing ministry your way—the way *God* intends for you—take your sixth suitcase with you to church!

## REFLECTIONS FOR YOUR JOURNEY

1. a. What are the most urgent needs for help in your church right now?

   b. How could you use your talent strengths to help meet these needs?

2. a. What is the biggest hindrance to your beginning a new ministry through your church?

   b. What needs to occur in order for you to overcome this obstacle?

3. Elisha served Elijah for several years before beginning an independent ministry (1 Kings 19:19-21, 2 Kings 2:1-15). How might you serve as an apprentice in your area of interest as a step toward your ultimate ministry plan?

*For Group Discussion*
4. Share with each other the ministry plan you created in this chapter. Don't worry about how complete it is. Offer encouragement and suggestions to each other.

5. Share with each other your concerns or apprehensions about involvement in church ministry. Discuss practical ways to overcome these obstacles.

6. Choose one member's ministry plan and role play its presentation to church leadership.

# NINE

# HOBBIES—ARE YOU HAVING FUN YET?

nce you've learned how to apply your talent strengths in the major areas of relationships, work, and ministry outreach, you've learned how to eat your cake and have it too.

But the icing on the cake of your sixth suitcase application can be a new outlook on hobbies—a way of spending your free time expressing yourself according to how God has gifted you.

We'll be looking at recreational activities and hobbies as expressions of your talent strengths. We hope you'll find ways to develop the person God has equipped you to be.

## ARE YOU HAVING FUN YET?

We don't want you to analyze your hobbies to death and turn your discretionary time into an official time management project. We don't want to turn you into a super sleuth who carefully calculates every move every minute of the day, every day of the week, according to your talents. You'll drive yourself and everyone else around you nuts.

The approach we want you to take in this area is the "because I like it" approach. In your activities and hobbies you ought to have fun for fun's sake (assuming you're defining "fun" in a wholesome and healthy way).

If you have activities and hobbies that give you enjoyment and pleasure, by all means continue doing them. Most likely the reason you're having fun is that these outlets allow you to use the strengths God has given you.

But sometimes we can get caught up in activities that become a source of strain rather than relaxation. Golfing, for example, can deteriorate to anxiety about improving handicaps, pressure to wear the right clothes, nail-chewing over belonging to the "right" country club. That's not the kind of pastime that is going to help you grow as a person.

Others force themselves to join chambers of commerce or business organizations in an effort at self-improvement. But if they're trying to enhance a skill they don't naturally possess, they're swimming against the current. We've run into people who have spent years in public speaking clubs because they think it will help them advance in their job—but all they've accomplished is developing a high tolerance for the tremendous amount of stress that they experience when preparing to speak.

If you find yourself in this kind of situation, get yourself out of it. Don't punish yourself in your discretionary time by trying to improve in a way God never intended.

Think about your current activities and hobbies. Choose the ones that capture your imagination, that enrich and refresh you every time. You are having fun in these. Keep doing them.

If you can't think of any activities you're now involved in that nurture you, it's time to take a fresh look at hobbies. Too many people yield to pressure from family, friends, or employers in using up their leisure time. Are you just doing things others expect you to do?

A fresh look at discretionary time is especially critical if your evaluation of work revealed low compatibility in your current job. Your participation in church and in extracurricular activities will become your primary source for personal growth and the expression of your God-given talents. It's *your* free time—use it to the max.

The following exercise will help you evaluate how you are spending your free time.

## EXERCISE: A LOOK AT YOUR ACTIVITIES

1. In the space below, list the current activities you engage in during discretionary time. Include those that are purely for your enjoyment: for example, reading, walking, volunteer service, going to concerts or museums or zoos, craft projects, watching television, playing board games, window-shopping, garage sale browsing, vacations, small group participation. . . .

2. Go back to chapter 1 and review your list of your ten most enjoyable experiences. Select activities you would like to try again—even if you wouldn't know how to do or have not had the time to start them up again.

*Examples:* the drama club you were a part of in high school; the choir touring group that you participated in during college; the art class that you enjoyed; the ham radio building kit that you completed; the debate team on which you competed. . . .

3. Now list activities you have dreamed about doing but have never done—perhaps because you didn't know how to get started or have not had the time or money.

If you can't immediately think of anything, leaf through your local newspaper's weekly entertainment guide and review the different activities offered. Try not to allow the habitual patterns and criticism of your immediate circle of family or friends to limit your daydreaming at this point.

4. Now compare your current activities (question 1) to your past or potential desired activities (questions 2 and 3). Are there any activities you would like to shift to your current list? Don't make any decisions right now; just answer hypothetically. This is only a paper exercise to give you freedom to consider how you might stretch your personal growth and talent expression through your hobbies.

   If you do have any possible changes in mind, note them here:

5. In chapter 8, we introduced some creative approaches to looking at your ministry in the local church. Is there any way you could channel hobbies or free-time activities through your church? Perhaps it would involve the participation or support of other members, or coordination with other community churches. Jot down any ideas you have about accomplishing this integration.

## EXPLORING NEW OPTIONS

Any changes in activities or hobbies will require some degree of boldness as you step out in a new direction.

The most critical talent that will impact your boldness and capacity to take a risk is your *relational* talent.

*Multi-Relationals:* The thought of reaching out to a new activity or social group is not a problem. More than likely you already know someone who is involved in your targeted area.

However, if you have a spouse who is not *multi-relational*, be sensitive. You can be a tremendous asset to your spouse in making a transition, but don't impose your *relational* strength; just make it an available resource.

*Familiar Group Relationals:* Your transition to other activities will take some effort. You probably have a tendency to stay with your usual associations. Your participation in group identity may mean that you value established relationships over new activities.

To demonstrate excellence in how God has gifted you, you may have to break some traditions with a familiar circle of friends. We suggest that you do not notify the group when you're in this process of change. Try out new areas for three to six months before you decide to drop a familiar activity. Sometimes it's helpful to explore new opportunities with a good friend who would also like to sample them. Don't let your loyalty to an established group inhibit your growth.

*Singular Relationals:* The thought of changing current activities, which are centered around people you know, can be threatening. Consider this kind of change carefully. The easiest way to proceed with a change will be to recruit a close friend or your spouse to this new activity—assuming they have a similar desire.

Another approach is to conduct an information-gathering interview with someone currently involved in the activity you're considering. For example, let's assume you are considering volunteering your time at the local municipal library, but you don't know anyone and you don't even know if they use volunteers. Make an appointment to interview the library director, or the reference librarian, to get more information. Try this first rather than presenting yourself as a volunteer.

You could also consult reading material, or family and friends who might be experienced in this area, to familiarize yourself with the activity and boost your confidence.

*Singular relationals* have a tendency to stay on familiar ground and not venture off into uncharted areas. So be prepared for surprises, but realize that this is an opportunity for you to grow and develop as a person.

In addition to accounting for your *relational* strength, check your current or desired hobbies against your *communication* and *functional* strengths as well. And be on guard against dabbling: trying things here and there but never making a decision and sticking with it long enough to find out if it's the right area for you. For your strengths to grow, commitment to the right activities is necessary. Extracurricular activities will allow you to do that. Dabbling will not.

## THE BENEFITS OF HOBBIES
## THAT USE YOUR NATURAL STRENGTHS

As a major diversion from mid-career-transition counseling, John enjoys being out in the wilderness. He communes with nature, listens to the rushing water, and smells the forest air; he speaks out loud to God. He finds it tremendously renewing and refreshing.

John's outdoor adventures are not immediately tied to one particular talent strength. He is *familiar group relational,* but the solitude he enjoys outdoors allows him to reflect back on his work, which is his primary place for expressing his natural abilities. Most of his time in the woods is spent letting his thoughts wander with him over the terrain and reevaluating things that went on during his week.

Being out in the woods allows John to clean his slate mentally, making room for his imagination to run free.

John's other identity is "Buffalo Jack." In the woods he sees himself as a seventeenth-century mountain man roaming the hills. That's part of the renewal process for him: he's not stuck in the grind of limitations that his job imposes on him.

After this description of his favorite activity, it might surprise you to learn that John does *not* have *functional* strengths in *observing details* of the physical environment or in *physical coordination*. On the other hand, he has a vivid imagination, some *acting* talent, and resolves problems of a theoretical nature. He simply loves being outdoors, and he uses this activity to complement the intensity of his work, where he concentrates most of his personal growth and development.

Jay, on the other hand, a former professional basketball player, does have a *physical coordination* talent strength. He puts it to good work in his recreational hobby of vigorous exercise—basketball with the guys, tennis or racquetball with friends, or a solitary jog. For Jay, working up a good sweat and turning his endorphins loose leaves him feeling ready to take on the world.

Jay also has a *creative* strength. Some of his best creative times occur after working out. They usually take place when he's driving late at night, alone or with everyone asleep in the car. So, in a way, driving late at night has become one of Jay's pleasurable activities.

Like John, Jay exercises his natural talents at his job, where he is fortunate to be doing a little better than sixty-forty. Exercise and daydreaming are also complementary extracurricular activities for him.

One classic change Jay and John have witnessed, in which a person dramatically changed her extracurricular activities and to some extent her lifestyle as well, involved an elementary school teacher named Marion.

Marion went home each night from teaching second grade stressed out. Normal classroom challenges left her with little energy. She spent most evenings and weekends with friends or at church, "relaxing" to get ready for another week.

Marion's one big event each year was a two-week vacation in Palm Springs, doing nothing but reading and sitting by the pool.

Then Marion began to realize that her work did not give her opportunity for personal growth (the sixty-forty principle was reversed for her, to forty-sixty). Instead of quitting her job, Marion began to explore new activities that would use her natural talents. At a friend's encouraging, she enrolled in tennis lessons at a community college. After three quarters she graduated to a tennis club.

Now, as a tennis club member, Marion enjoys not only the new challenge of using her *physical coordination* talent, but also a new network of friends as well. It took time for her to reach this level of participation, but it was well worth it.

Look for activities that are enjoyable and bring you a sense of renewal and refreshment rather than status, association with "important" people, or a fad. Commit yourself to the time, finances, and training that might be necessary; seek to be an accomplished, skilled person in your hobby or activity rather than a dabbler. Like John, Jay, and Marion, you may find that it opens up a whole new world to you.

## REFLECTIONS FOR YOUR JOURNEY

1. Study the following passages: Romans 14:1-23, 1 Corinthians 6:12, Colossians 3:1-17. What guidelines can you find in these scriptures for determining what kinds of hobbies or activities are appropriate for Christians?

2. Write down what you feel to be the most important benefits of hobbies or free time activities.

3. Do you plan to make any changes in how you use your discretionary time? If so, describe what they are and any steps you need to take to implement them.

*For Group Discussion*

4. Discuss with each other how examining your talent strengths affected your view of hobbies and free time, as well as any changes you plan to make.

5. There are numerous community service and ministry organizations as well as local church programs in desperate need of volunteers. Keeping this in mind, discuss the question, "How much of my free time could I use *helping others* while using my talent strengths?"

# TEN

# GO FOR IT!

hat makes the difference between "good" athletes and those who make it to the top of their field to become professionals? Our experience with professional athletes in basketball, football, and baseball has given us an insight into this question.

These pro players all have, of course, superior *physical coordination* talent in addition to other talent strengths. But they also share another characteristic, something beyond aptitude or being in the right place at the right time. This element is their key to breaking through to a high level of achievement in their respective sports:

*They have disciplined themselves to focus their attention on a task in which they have committed themselves to excellence.*

171

They marshal all of their energy, thought, and concentration on that one activity in order to master it.

This is what it takes for all of us to achieve a level of excellence in our lifetime: a concentrated focus on our natural talent strengths. Too often we try to excel in areas for which we lack natural talent. We need to develop the resources God has given us, believe in them, and believe that He is honored in our accomplishments through them.

## A FRESH LOOK

Remember when we asked you in the introduction to name three people you admired for their accomplishments? We challenged you to consider that you could be as good in your field as they are in theirs.

How did you feel about that challenge? How do you feel about it now, *after* reading this book? We hope you've taken a fresh look at your potential and become encouraged by the possibilities.

Possibilities—just think of them, if *all* of God's people were growing in the way God had gifted them, if they were meeting their challenges in life in a positive way, if they were acting interdependently with others. We wouldn't need so many sophisticated evangelism campaigns. Spiritually hungry nonbelievers would be beating a path to our door for the secret that allowed us to be at peace with ourselves and our fellow human beings. The world would stand in awe of the discipline with which we lived our lives. They would beg to know our secrets.

You should now be aware of ample opportunities to make a contribution *just the way you are*. We have encouraged you to excel at something to be an example, to be influential. We've tried to give you new insights for ministry through your local church and for creative use of hobbies and recreational time. We've encouraged you to look at relationships in a new way and evaluate how well your work life is tapping into your talents.

Individuals who have not identified and developed their God-given strengths will soon grow frustrated with their lot in life. They may even drift away from the Creator who lovingly fashioned them for His purposes.

## ADVICE FOR THE ROAD

We'd like to give you some closing advice for the road—traveling tips for taking your sixth suitcase with you on the journey of life.

We've divided these tips into three categories: mapping out your change strategy; negotiating for success; and overcoming obstacles.

## MAPPING OUT YOUR CHANGE STRATEGY

These suggestions are to help you carry out the kinds of changes we've urged you toward in chapters 6 through 9.

1. *Before initiating any change in your life, pray about it.* Pray for yourself as well as those with whom you will be sharing your plans. Pray repeatedly, as often as you think about the change you are planning. This is the most important ingredient. Don't leave it out.

2. *Outline in written form what you plan to do, step by step.*

3. *Write out a word-for-word script of your proposed change.* Include everything you plan to say to the person(s) who are a part of your plan.

4. *Record your script on audio cassette.* Listen to it, review your content and delivery, and re-record it until it sounds natural.

5. *Ask someone to critique your presentation.* Have a friend or your study group listen to your audio cassette and give you feedback. Make revisions as necessary.

6. *Meet with the person you have selected to share your planned change.* This should be the person who will benefit from your change, or whose authority or support or partici-

pation you are seeking. Feed the results back to your friends or the members of your study group.

## NEGOTIATING FOR SUCCESS

These ideas are to help you succeed in implementing your planned changes. The process of negotiation involves *what you need to do in order to gain support and build momentum for your ideas*. You'll find that these principles apply primarily to the areas of work and ministry (chapters 7 and 8), where you're more likely to need approval or authority.

1. *Take an informal survey of responses to your ideas.* Ask five to ten influential people to give you their opinion on the changes you're planning. Don't spend more than five minutes with each person. Ask simply, "I've been thinking about this—what do you think?"

Your primary objective in this survey is to get feedback that will enable you later to propose your ideas in final form as effectively as possible.

A secondary objective in the survey is to collect endorsements. If you can cite positive responses to your ideas when making your official presentation, you will improve the chances of getting a go-ahead from supervisory authority.

Depending upon the extent of the changes you plan, you might also consider a more formal survey, such as a questionnaire going out to two hundred or more people. Include questions such as "How do you feel about the need for [your idea]?—(a) positive, (b) neutral, (c) negative" and so forth. Leave space for comments.

An extended survey such as this can provide a wealth of information and suggestions, credibility to back up your proposal, and publicity for your ideas (you'll get everyone talking).

2. *Conduct an informal interview with the person who needs to approve your idea.* Look for that teacher, manager, pastor, committee head, or official who has the authority to endorse your plan. If there is more than one person, you

may need to duplicate this technique with others.

If you don't know the person who will be approving your plan, perhaps you could ask a friend of yours who is close to that individual to arrange a meeting. Whether you or a friend makes the appointment, set up this exploratory meeting in an informal atmosphere.

During this informal interview, ask that authority person what his or her feelings would be about the plan you're considering. Get input by asking questions: "What are your greatest concerns regarding this proposal?" "What have you tried in the past that has worked, and what has not worked?"

Don't request approval for your idea at this initial meeting. As you gather information, take notes so that later you can use the same wording to express your ideas and plan. It will enable that person to understand you more easily when you are officially requesting permission or support.

Based upon the information you learn in this interview, you should know what new support data to collect, what strategic plan you will need, and how to communicate that you have a great idea. Before you go back to this person with your official proposal, review your findings with your group for their suggestions.

3. *For church ministry plans, recruit a spokesperson to make presentations for you.* Enlisting someone to speak for you is advisable even if you have strong abilities in *giving presentations,* because the creator of a plan often tends to talk too long about it. If you don't have strong presentation talents, you're taking a big risk doing it yourself. Most people won't look beyond first impressions to examine the actual content.

Recruit someone who is good at addressing an audience and ask him or her to present your plan to a Sunday school class, the Wednesday evening assembly, or any other church meeting. Plan to be there as well to answer questions.

4. *Find a gifted promoter who will champion your plan.*

This promoter doesn't necessarily have to engage in *speaking in public*. There are a variety of other ways to inspire confidence and support for your idea. Even a simple plug every now and then—"I think this plan will be a great help to us"—can move your ideas forward. If you try to do it, you may be perceived as boastful or just pushy about your own interests.

5. *Conduct a pilot project that includes the decision-maker(s) or other influential people.* If your idea is a long-term venture, then suggest a one-time sampler.

Get written evaluations from all the people who participate in your pilot program. Have them write out what they liked and suggest improvements. Often the pilot experience helps the participant realize a potential obstacle was really not a problem.

If your negotiating techniques fail to get the support you need, perhaps your idea needs further work. If you've taken all the steps above, you'll probably find out where the weaknesses are.

But sometimes you'll run up against resistance that doesn't seem to have any clear reasons. People may mask their objections with phrases such as, "Management won't approve it." "It's too political." "It's just not appropriate for our denomination." "We didn't have time to discuss it in the committee meeting." Or even, "We're praying about it."

If you experience long delays in getting a decision as well as negative comments, look for evidence of one of the obstacles listed in the next section.


## OVERCOMING OBSTACLES TO CHANGE

When you plan a change, you should expect to encounter roadblocks in your path. They come with the territory.

There's no way for you to eliminate obstacles, but that doesn't mean you can't get past them. With sufficient motivation and commitment to your goals, you can go through, around, and over them.

Dr. James Dobson's strong advice to parents in his book *Hide or Seek* applies here. To overcome the obstacle of inferiority, he encourages moms and dads to compel their children to excel in some activity early. (His father compelled him to master tennis.) This training can teach children to grow through confronting obstacles rather than avoiding them.

The best way to handle obstacles is to understand them and meet them head on. The following obstacles are the ones you're most likely to face as you put your plans into action (especially in those areas you explored in chapters 7 through 9).

*Resistance to Novelty*

When others hear your plan, expect comments like "I've never heard of this before" or "We've never done it that way." This is a very common reaction to something new. People will hesitate to react positively just because the idea is different. Their reaction is not a reflection on the merit of your idea. It's simply a response to novelty.

We can illustrate this by imagining that our children have just made a novel request: they want a pig to keep as a pet. Most of us have never considered this before. We react negatively right away—"they stink," or "you can't housetrain them." The fact is, most of us do not have enough information to make an informed response. So we take the safe route: "I know about dogs and cats, not about pigs. So let's get a dog or a cat and forget the pig idea."

When you realize that most people tend to resist change just because it means accepting the new and unknown, you can prepare yourself. Expect to take time to introduce your plan. The first time people hear about it, it's novel. The second time, it's a possibility. The third time around it achieves the status of a consideration. And let's hope that by the fourth or fifth, it's met with enthusiasm as a great idea.

It is amazing how many people will present an idea only once and then sit back and wait for others to embrace it. They adopt the attitude, "They know about it, and they know where to reach me." But Moses didn't go to Pharaoh and demand, "Let my people go!" on only one occasion. He went *ten times*.

With the help of your group or feedback person, you can come up with additional ways to present your idea. Repetition often removes the novelty obstacle.

### Desire to Preserve the Status Quo

Every group, company, family and church has a traditional way of doing things. This is the status quo. And wherever you find the status quo, you'll find a desire to preserve it. This is the corollary of resistance to novelty.

People will want to know how the plan you're recommending is going to fit. Oh, maybe they won't ask you point blank, but they will want to know if it will disrupt or support their habitual patterns.

If your idea is perceived as a threat to the status quo, you can count on opposition. To combat this obstacle, consider what traditions are important to others and how your ideas can be presented in a way that supports those traditions. If the status quo is part of what you want to change, present your ideas as an *improvement* on traditions so you don't give the impression that you are simply out to attack and replace them.

### Urgent Priorities

Sometimes your plans may be in competition with urgent priorities that are already in place.

Leaders or supervisors are often preoccupied with these priorities. They may ask you why you want to act on your plan instead of helping them meet more urgent needs. What should you do if this happens?

First, give prayerful consideration to volunteering to work in one of these areas. Sometimes it is godly to say

"Yes" to their request; sometimes it is godly to say "No."

When you put your plan on hold and give your efforts to alleviate a pressing need, we recommend you make sure the leaders understand what you are doing, why, and how long you will be available. It is important for the long haul that your contribution utilizes your natural strengths.

From time to time it's appropriate to help out by doing jobs that nobody else wants to do. But in the life span of your participation in your church, club, family, or organization, your unique contribution should be given serious attention.

### Habitual Expectations

If you have been in your organization very long you probably have established a reputation for being a certain kind of person or doing certain kinds of things. When you're around others long enough, they get in the habit of expecting certain things from you.

If your proposal places you in a different role, you can anticipate that others will be slow to warm up to the idea. Their habitual expectations of you will get in the way of their ability to envision you making the new contribution. This is a variation of the novelty obstacle, in which people confront a plan they never before considered. Here, even if your plan involves familiar activities, people are confronting a "you" they never thought of before.

Once again, it will take time and repetition to overcome this obstacle.

### The Appearance of Duplication

If you're proposing something that is similar to what's already being done, others may think there's no need for your plan. It may appear that you are simply duplicating effort.

Do *not* work up a case for why your way is better. This strategy will not win friends, influence people, or gain approval for you.

*Do* focus your idea sharply enough to show that it is specialized. Emphasize how it is different or unique and therefore will complement rather than duplicate.

*Expenses*
Things tend to slow down when you have to go before a budget committee and get an appropriation of funds to launch your plan. Someone goes on vacation and there isn't a quorum. A subcommittee chairperson in your field is down with the flu. The decision keeps getting delayed.

When you ask for money, there will be twice as much scrutiny and hassle in getting approval. Implementation always takes longer when expenses are required.

Our best advice is to plan on financing your pilot activities out of your own pocket. And if possible, find independent resources to finance the continuation of your plan so you will not be dependent upon allocations and budgets. If your idea is so extensive that you are not able to finance it yourself, figure out how to reduce expenses.

Above all, don't resent any problems you encounter. God delights in eliminating obstacles. Remember Daniel in the lion's den, David facing Goliath, and Elijah confronting the six hundred prophets of Baal. If you believe in your proposed idea and you have confirmation from your advisors, you should persevere.

## AND NOW, GO FOR IT

God has uniquely gifted you, and there will be many opportunities in your life in which you can choose to hone and polish that capacity for excellence. Discovery of those opportunities sometimes comes by accident, but mostly it comes by planned, purposeful thinking.

We hope this book has helped you to discover opportunities. But the honing and polishing of your sixth suitcase aptitude is up to you: it requires your thorough determination. When you admire others' feats of achievement, remember how much time and attention they gave to their activity.

It's one thing to imagine change; it's another thing to implement it. Both Jay and John are initiators. We are change agents. God has designed us in our own unique ways to encourage change, to build, develop, motivate, and introduce. We want to motivate you to act. We want you to be a success story in your community and church as an example for others.

Five frogs are on a log. Four decide to jump. How many are left?

Five—because deciding to jump and jumping are two separate actions. Actually, jumping validates the strength of the decision to jump.

As you have worked through this material you have probably made some decisions. Just remember, what you do next will validate the strength of your decisions. If you have decided to jump, then jump! You'll find that you've landed on your own personal path to excellence.

## REFLECTIONS FOR YOUR JOURNEY

1. What are the two greatest insights you have gained from this book?

2. Review the suggestions in these sections from this chapter: "Mapping Out Your Change Strategy," "Negotiating for Success," and "Overcoming Obstacles to Change." Write down any ideas you can find in this material that are specifically helpful for the kinds of practical changes you desire to make—whether in relationships, work, ministry, or free time.

3. a. If you could sit down with John Bradley and Jay Carty for a personal conversation, what questions would you ask them?

   b. Can anyone in your church, study group, or community help you answer these questions? Write down who they are and what you would ask them.

4. What are three goals you would most like to accomplish in order to develop your talent strengths and make better use of them in your everyday life?

   a.

   b.

   c.

*For Group Discussion*

5. Discuss your responses to the questions in this section. Review gains and needs for improvement in your personal growth that have been stimulated by this book.

6. Would anyone in your group like to lead another group through *Discovering Your Natural Talents* in the future? Brainstorm ideas for recruiting group members. Review what has worked well in your group, as well as ideas for improvement in future sessions.